Dear
Nasreen,

"Doubt kills

dreams than failure
ever will"

Best Wishes

Ujana Ayg

My New Journey

My Letters To You

Urfana Ayub

Adam Ayub Publications

My Inspiration
Adam Ayub

"Your deepest pain can become your biggest strength"

Urfana Ayub

Dedication

This book consists of letters which I am dedicating to my very dear and beloved son, the late Muhammad Adam Ayub. By giving birth to Adam, I became a mother for the very first time and experienced the unique sentiments of motherhood. Adam's life enlightened my life and his death opened doors of insight into the lives of many others. His role in my life was that of a very fine teacher. The Creator Allah (SWT) blessed Adam's short life with many favours. Today, by the grace of Allah (SWT), Adam lives in the hearts of not only his mother and family members, but also in thehearts of many other people Alhamdulilah.

Urfana Ayub

Surah
Al-Baqarah
(The Cow) 2:201

رَبَّنَا آتِنَا فِي الدُّنْيَا حَسَنَةً وَفِي الْآخِرَةِ حَسَنَةً وَقِنَا عَذَابَ النَّارِ

Translation: In the name of Allah the most
Merciful the most Benevolent

"O our lord, grant us good in this world and
good in the hereafter and save us from the
torment of hellfire."

Sentiments and Reflections

'My Letters to You', Urdu title *"Maray Khat Taray Naam"*, was first published in September 2015 in the Urdu language, attracting many messages of praise from readers worldwide.

"You have given voice to my feelings."

Saeeda

"A book of self reflection and self analysis."

Khaliq

"Reading this book was like reading my heart. It mirrored so many of my inner thoughts. One is able to relate to it in some way or another. The Ayahs of the Quran and Hadith applied to specific situations, allowing the reader to contemplate and benefit from self-reflection and analysis. I found that issues I wanted to voice, but not always had the courage to with regards to our society's failure of applying the beautiful law of Allah and Sunnah of our beloved Prophet (S.A.W.), had clearly yet subtly been conveyed through the letters. Overall, a very good book which I will be sharing with others, In Sha Allah".

Zeenat

"Maray Khat Taray Naam" is full of guidance for readers and hope for humanity."

Jameel

"A mother's reflection and attempt to seek resolution and acceptance to her greatest loss. This book is thought provoking, intellectually stimulating and a brilliant attempt to resolve and accept Allah's (SWT) will. Your grief will always be there, however your dedication and commitment to turn a huge loss into meaning through your intellect and creativity is very believable. Readers will have to read this book a few times to sense the true gravity and meaning and the laudable attempts to seek the bigger meaning of our being, our connections with the Creator, what is important and what matters! And what is not. The need is to reflect and change".

Amina

"This book is a great source of comfort, support and strength to cope. This book has taught me a lesson, which is - It's not what we say, it's the way we say it. This leaves a profound effect on people. Urfana has proved in *"Maray khat Taray Naam"* that she has the talent to convey the most difficult issues of society in a very simple and subtle way."

Ahsan

"I wish this book were written in English so I could read the full book, together with many others who wish to read. I could only read the English section from *"Maray khat Taray Naam"* My letters to you. You are an inspiration to us. I do feel your pain just as I felt my sister's pain when she lost her son."

Anonymous

"The whole concept and idea of two books is a great way of getting such beautiful messages out there for all readers which we can relate to, learn from and reflect on. I read both your books and both are very well written; the two books are similar yet so different. I would like to say

"Maray Khat Taray Naam" gives readers many lessons

and advice on how to reflect and live our lives in a better way. It contains many useful tips and duas for all the readers to help better themselves for this life and the next."

Hina

"I have read the book and I loved it. This book may seem as though it's a biography at first, but it is not. In fact it is a journey that shows the life of the writer both from outside and inside. She expresses her experience in an easy way by using simple language that shows her true feelings. The writer uses the sorrow of her son's death to help people in a positive way socially, psychologically and emotionally, enabling the welfare of the readers. Also showing ways to keep away from the negativity in life and what can lead you astray. This is a read that helps one to become a better person, containing lessons on morality and spirituality. This book is worth a read to help readers to lead a simple, blissful and peaceful life. May Allah give Adam the highest place in Heaven, and may Allah give Urfana strength to keep writing books to help others."

Shahnaz

"**My Letters to You** is an open invitation for people to reflect, analyse and contemplate. It teaches readers to be grateful to Allah in every situation. The teaching of Islam and humanity is fragranced in this book for readers to learn lessons from daily living examples."

Almas

Contents

Preface

I belong to Karachi, a beautiful city of Pakistan. After getting married I moved over to England in 1990. Alhamdulilah, Allah(SWT) blessed me with four children. My life was passing smoothly when all of a sudden it changed and 27th December 2009 became the most important day of my life for multiple reasons. This day left my life with a vacuum which was created by the departure of the person who made me a mother for the very first time, Praise be to Allah. He was my friend, my companion, my well-wisher and also my firstborn. He was only 18 years old. He was my son Muhammad Adam Ayub. Adam Ayub was the source of much happiness for our family, as the first grandson on both the maternal and paternal sides and a favourite with everybody.

Adam was born with a heart problem. He was a blue baby at birth. He had his first heart surgery at the age of one and then open heart surgery at the tender age of five. He stayed in intensive care for some time and Praise be to Allah he survived this major heart surgery and Allah (SWT) gave him new life.

Being our first child, everyone adored him. I then had three more healthy children, Arslan, Ambar and Ahmad.

Everyone always gave Adam special treatment, love and respect for who he was. He was very close to his family here in UK and his maternal family in Pakistan.

Adam seemed to be progressing very well with his usual checkups at Leeds General Infirmary. He had just started a

Youth and Community degree course in September 2009 in Leeds. But during his Christmas holidays he fell ill with stomach pains. At first we thought it was just a normal illness and nothing major to worry about. But after a few days Adam was still not eating, therefore on December 26th, he went to the hospital to get it checked out. He finished watching his football match and left home with me and his father without hugging his siblings or saying formal goodbyes, thinking he would be back soon.

But he never came home again. Adam died the next morning in hospital from pneumonia with his family at his side. We were all in shock, as Adam's father and I had never witnessed any death in our lives. This was so sudden and Adam was just 18 years old with a life full of promise.

Adam's departure opened my eyes to many things. My child had the best of manners and the best of character. His smile adorned his face. His quiet passing created a bond between me, death, funeral and the grave. Alhamdolilah, he made me aware of the Hereafter. It is for this reason that I am so very grateful and indebted to my child Adam Ayub. It is my fervent prayer that the lesson I learnt from this extraordinary and unforgettable experience may never fade from my memory. To learn something spiritual or be taught by Allah (SWT) is a divine gift, even if it is the result of a bereavement and heartache! Alhamdolilah I learnt a lot from Adam's departure. I realised what we cannot learn from books.

I started writing after Adam, and put down my experiences and emotions on paper which led to the birth of my first book *Taray Janay Kay Baad (After You Were Gone)*, which tells the story of Adam's passing and my first year after he departed from this earth. People who read this book encouraged me to write again. I hope that, as people found **Taray Janay Kay Baad** useful and learnt something from it, similarly *"My Letters To You"* will also give them reason to meditate. Even if a single thing in this book makes an impact upon you, please share it with those around you so that it may become a source of Sadaqa e Jariya (source of eternal reward) for you.

I am grateful from the depth of my heart to all those who helped me at any stage of this book. I pray that Allah (SWT) may make *"My Letters To You"* a source of a permanent reward for us all, Ameen. My message is *"learn to live for others"*. It is no big deal to live for one's own self. The entire system of nature teaches us the same lesson and invites us to think about it.

A river does not drink its own water, the sun does not benefit from its radiance and flowers spread their fragrance for others. We must also strive to please Allah (SWT). We should try to help others selflessly in life without expecting any reward in return. Love people only for Allah's sake, without any greed or selfishness. Expect reward only from your Sustainer and Creator who will, In Sha Allah, reward you with the best gift ever. You only have to make up your mind, the options will automatically open up for you and you will, In Sha Allah, reach your destination.

I also pray that may Allah (SWT) makes us non-dependent on other people and keep us connected always with Him, Ameen. Through this book I would like to thank my parents, my in-laws, my children and my husband whose absolute love, encouragement and trust gave me the confidence to embark on this project. After reading this book, if you want to give me your valuable feedback, please contact me at this email address:

Email: *adamayubbooks@gmail.com*

With best wishes and prayers,

Urfana Ayub

Letter No 1.

My first letter to you

My dearest son Adam Ayub,
Peace be upon you.

My dear child, today after a long time I have dared to pick up my pen again. It is not that I have not thought about you. You are always in my thoughts. I did not forget you for even a moment. As a poet said:

> *My mind is reserved only for your memory*
> *No need to remember you as I never forget you*

Adam today is ninth Muharram. Five years ago on ninth Muharram you spent the last day of your life with your family members. Today sitting in my room, I am thinking of that last day when you were with us. When you were breathing the air of this world, and then suddenly on the morning of tenth Muharram you left us all and went back to your Creator.

Many times during these five years I felt a strong desire to talk to you, to write to you and tell you how I spent those five years. Where has life brought me to? But I could not write despite wanting to. Why? I don't know. There are some questions and decisions to which there are no answers and no explanations. Now I have made up my mind that I will Insha'Allah keep contact with you through these letters.

First of all, tell me how are you? In the world of my mind you are Masha'Allah, a tall, happy, well built and a healthy young man. I know that you are in the protection of my Sustainer and are peaceful and content. Allhamduliah (*praise be to Allah*) I am content too.

Your father, Arslan, Ambar, Ahmad and myself are fine and we are missing you. Dadi Jan, Baba, your Phuphie Farhat, all your Chachas, Aunties and their children, miss you. Also in Pakistan, Nani Jan, Nana Abba, all your Mamoons and Aunties and their children miss you a lot and talk about you in their daily routine. Nobody has forgotten you. The neighbours' children, your friends and all the people who knew you always talk about you whenever they meet us. An interesting thing is that people still recognize me through your reference, that is, as Adam's mother. None of them refer to me as Arslan's or Ahmad's mother. Maybe people talk about mothers through reference to their firstborn. I like it when people introduce me as Adam's mother.

Adam, there are a lot of things which I want to talk to you about, but I cannot write all my experiences of five years in a single letter. So I have decided to continue writing to you and remain in contact. This is a beginning of a new journey for me. May Allah (SWT) guide me and make all the things easy for me, Ameen.

I leave you in the protection of Allah (SWT) who is the ultimate master and creator. Though I cannot comprehend His wisdom, I fully believe in it. May Allah (SWT) be your guardian, my son.

Allah Hafiz.

Your Mother,
Urfana Ayub

21

Success in this world and in the hereafter

Dear son Adam Ayub,
Peace be upon you.

As a poet said:

My mind is in anticipation of the sound of someone's footsteps
My sight is yearning for a face
Though I am not in want of anything after you
But after you I am heavy hearted all the time

My dearest son it is tenth of Muharram today. Five years ago at eight a.m. on tenth Muharram you left this world. That day and those moments are engraved in my memory. There are certain days when I feel very depressed, like for example today, on Eid and on any happy or sad occasion when the whole family gathers. On such occasions my eyes keep seeking you as if I might suddenly see you among the gathering of people. It is also strange how our minds and sentiments somehow acknowledge the worldly calendar and become melancholy on specific days and months.

But having said all this, I do not mean that I am unhappy or I have not accepted your going away. I have fully accepted Allah's wisdom and decision with all my heart because it is Allah's (SWT) will. May Allah (SWT) grant patience to me and to all those relatives who loved you dearly, Ameen. Your sudden death was such a shock for me which changed my whole life. It gave a new meaning and purpose to my life. Now I can clearly perceive all those basic realities about this world, life and death which were indistinct to me before. Now there are no doubts in my mind. I have finally understood the status of a human being and I have also learnt the grace and magnificence of Almighty Allah (SWT).

What is this world? Now I can see the deception behind it What is death? Now I can perceive its reality.

After your departure I put down my sentiments and emotions on paper in book form and *Taray Janay Kay Baad (After You Were Gone)* came into existence. I wrote this book and it contains your fragrance and your being. It contains my agony and your memories. Above all, this book was a means to thank Allah (SWT) who gave you to me, made me a mother and thus placed me at the highest status of mankind. And then very suddenly, but lovingly and gracefully, he called you back from this world.

You know Adam, I had never written before and neither did I know how to write. Writing my thoughts after you was a means that provided strength and support to me. I decided to convert this into a book. Praise be to Allah (SWT), by the grace of Allah (SWT), *"After You Were Gone"* was published in April 2011.

The book is proving to be a source of endless reward for you. It has collected lots of good deeds for you. It is assisting many deserving people and institutes. Insha'Allah this work will continue. I pray to Allah (SWT) that may He accept and endorse our endeavours and may Allah (SWT) give the best of rewards to me and all those who bought, read or helped in any stages of the completion of this book in any way, Ameen.

Adam, the book "After You Were Gone" opened new horizons in my life and revealed a new destination to me. I found new companions on this way. All these companions had experienced some trauma in life and Praise be to they found comfort and strength by reading this book. Adam, you linked me with the entire world. *"After You Were Gone"* embarked on a journey on its own from Pakistan to India and then to USA, Dubai, Canada, Switzerland and to so many other places!

When I started getting feedback from people by email, I was amazed to realise that you had become a part of so many people's lives and that you resided in so many different countries. Everyone remembers your name by heart Masha'Allah (whatever Allah wishes).

This book got a lot of recognition and praise. People gave you love and they seemed to know you without ever meeting you. You live on the bedside tables of these people. It is because of you that I became part of so many people's lives and sorrows. I saw and heard things which I might never have heard or felt if you had not gone away!

You are my teacher. Allah (SWT) has taught me many things through you, things pertaining to our religion and to this world also. You are still with me, walking by my side holding onto my hand, but now I feel it is the other way round. Now I am walking, holding onto your hand. I can feel your existence in this world near me. I am doing charity work in your name. You are talked about at every family gathering.

Even after your death you have not gone away. Adam, you live in our hearts. Your presence is more powerful, more tangible than many of those people who actually live on this earth. Even after your departure you are helping me in every aspect and decision of my life. I think of you whenever I make a decision. Your smiling face is always in my mind. Some people are not ours even though they live close to us. Masha'Allah you are close to our hearts even though you have gone beyond worldly boundaries. You are in our hearts and also in our homes. May Allah (SWT) give you the highest place in the hereafter and grant you a place in Jannat-ul-Firdous, Ameen.

Allah Hafiz.

Your Mother
Urfana Ayub

Letter No 3.

Our test

Dear son, my child Adam Ayub.
Peace be upon you.

Today, I went to the graveyard to meet you after a long time. As usual almost the entire graveyard was empty except for a few people present in a corner where probably a funeral was taking place. I went to your grave and prayed. I saw all the graves near yours and then drove around the whole graveyard in the car. There were only very few people that were present when I was there. The thought always strikes me *"why are graveyards so silent and deserted?"* The outside world is merry and boisterous. There is so much attraction in the outside world that it prevents man from even entering the graveyard lest he may start worrying for the Hereafter. Satan attacks man from every angle. You know Adam!

Five years ago there were graves on only one side of your grave and the other side was almost empty. Now it has been filled completely.

When we talk of populating or filling a graveyard, I instinctively think of those people's houses which were made desolate and empty because of the departure of their inhabitants. Only last night two teenage boys of about 18 or 20 years of age died in a car accident. They will also populate a graveyard and their houses will be left empty and deserted. When you were alive I was never so sensitive about other people's deaths, but since you went away it seems someone is dying every other day. It is not always the case that older people and the sick will die first. Now most of the time one is hearing about young deaths.

I met a friend's sister who had come from Pakistan. She asked me for a copy of your book *Taray Janay Kay Baad* for one of her friends. Then she told me about her friend's circumstances. Her friend was blessed with four healthy children, two sons and two daughters who died suddenly.

Her eldest son suddenly died in May 2009. In July 2010 her elder daughter died and then in January 2011 her third child, a girl, also died. After seeing three adolescent deaths, she went to perform Umrah with her youngest son who was sixteen years old. On her return flight from Umrah her fourth child too suddenly died.

Adam, theirs was a full household where four children grew up. The eldest son had done an MBA and the mother was preparing for his wedding. The older daughter was a doctor. The younger two children were still studying. In a short time span between 2009 and 2012, a happy, busy and full household became empty. I wonder what both of the parents would be going through. All the children were healthy. They did not have any prolonged illnesses. When Allah (SWT) summons someone, He does not need any excuse like illness or accident. Suddenly, without any reason, homes become vacant.

When only one person went away from our family, you, it felt as if the whole house had become empty. Arslan, Ambar and Ahmad can never make up for your absence. No love of any relative can replace you. It seems as if I have misplaced a very precious thing of mine. When our whole family performed Umrah after you, even then my eyes used to seek you, clad in an Ihram and doing Tawaf of Ka'aba. I used to pray that, though I know you are not here, still may Allah (SWT) let me see you doing Tawaf. Or maybe I catch sight of someone who looks like my Adam.

This was me who had lost only one son. How can I comprehend the grief of those parents who have lost all their four children, two grown up sons and two grown up daughters one after the other in a short span of time?

I heard that both parents have been very brave and have faced this grief with tremendous amount of courage. It is my heartiest prayer that Allah (SWT) may grant the parents and other relatives an abundance of patience. They have set up a trust in the name of their children, which will be a source of eternal reward for them. Both the parents are working honestly, courageously day and night to help the needy people. May Allah (SWT) accept their endeavours, Ameen.

I completely trust that my Sustainer will not put a burden on anyone beyond his or her limits. Whenever Allah (SWT) puts us to any test, I pray that may He keep us firm in our faith so that we can bear the difficulty with respect and grace. That is why it is said that a true Momin will find goodness and reward in every situation. When he is blessed, he is thankful to Allah (SWT) and when he is grieved, he practices patience. Thus he earns rewards from Allah (SWT) in both situations.

This is the way we should be. Our only desire should be a reward from Allah (SWT) and not sorrow or happiness, because the glamour of this world is nothing but deception. Sooner or later this is going to end. But the Hereafter is eternal; it will never end. With these feelings Adam, I trust you to the protection of Allah (SWT).

Allah Hafiz.

Your Mother,
Urfana Ayub

Letter No 4.

Alcohol – Mother of all the vices

Dear son, Adam.
Peace be upon you.

A new restaurant has opened in Bradford. Dad, your siblings and myself had been planning to visit it for the past few days. Today we went there. You know, Adam, that we do not like eating out much. The reality is that most of these restaurants serve alcohol. Non-Muslims like our Asian cuisine very much and they drink alcohol commonly. Muslim businessmen know very well that dealing with alcohol is a great sin, but still they serve alcohol to their non-Muslim customers in order to boost their trade.

The restaurant we visited today is very pretty. I had heard that they do not serve alcohol. That is why we went there. The food was delicious, the décor was exquisite and the ambience was very fine, but it was sad to see that apart from a few people, the restaurant was empty. I tried to figure out the reason behind this. Wasn't the food good? Wasn't there sufficient variety in the dishes? Was there any deficiency in the setting or quality of the restaurant? When Dad and I met the manager and asked him about the slow business, he said, *"We do not serve alcohol. I think this is the reason why so few customers come here."*

I was very pleased to meet the manager and I applauded his conviction and faith. He said, *"Many customers come to the restaurant, but when they find out that we do not allow alcohol in the restaurant, they leave."*

He also added that when booking halls for weddings, if the customers find out that they will not be permitted the use of alcohol during the ceremony, they cancel the bookings.

I told the manager that Allah (SWT) is testing his faith. Saying *"No"* to a customer shows that you have strong faith which makes you refuse. Most people let go of their faith in order to win petty worldly gains. He told us that his father says, *"Even if the income is meagre, it should be pure and blessed"*.

Masha'Allah, meeting such people rejuvenates my own faith. It shows that there are still such people out there who would not dare to displease Allah (SWT) for worldly benefits. This becomes all the more difficult when the whole world is doing it, and they think that the wrong action is correct since *"everybody is doing it"*. It is not necessary that what everybody is doing has to be correct.

May Allah (SWT) give us the ability to use our own analytical powers to differentiate right from wrong according to Allah's (SWT) commandments, no matter what the circumstances are and no matter what people are indulging in. Even if the entire world is on one side, and doing something wrong, we should have the faith and courage to stand up to the world and try our level best to please Allah (SWT). This temporary gain should not pollute our hearts and Imaan (faith), Ameen.

Adam, do you remember that before your departure I had started going to the city of Leeds? I attended a course to understand the Quran with full meaning and reference. Masha'Allah, after understanding the Quran, I have learnt that drinking alcohol, serving it, manufacturing it, selling it and dealing with it in any way is disliked by Allah (SWT) very much. In this regard, the Quran says:

"The Shaitan (Satan) desires only to put hatred and enmity among you through wine and gambling and to bar you from the remembrance of Allah and from Salah, will you not then desist?"

Surah Al-Ma'idah (The Table Spread) 5:91

Our beloved Prophet Hadrat Muhammad (PBUH) said,

"Alcohol is the mother of all the vices and is the most shameful of all bad things"

Sunnan Abi Maja

In another Hadeeth, Hadrat Muhammad (PBUH) said,

"Alcohol and faith (Imaan) cannot coexist"
Nisai

The first revelation in Quran regarding alcohol comes in Surah Al-Baqarah:

"They ask you about wine and gambling. Say, "In them is great sin and [though, some] benefit for people. But their sin is greater than their benefit."

Surah Al-Baqarah (The Cow) 2:219

I pray to Allah (SWT) that may He give guidance to all of us, including myself, and lead us to the right path. May He give us the ability to refrain from sins and prohibited things which are disliked by Allah (SWT). I also pray for the brother whom I met in the restaurant that may Allah (SWT) keep him steadfast in his religion and faith. Furthermore, may his business prosper and may Allah (SWT) keep him resolute on his decision in this competitive world (Ameen).

With love and prayers.

Allah Hafiz.

My Adam's mum

Letter No 5.

Are we prepared?

Dear son, Adam Ayub,
Peace be upon you.

How is my child today? I and all of your family members miss you a lot. Nobody has forgotten you. In the world of my heart you are growing every year. I often think that you went away so early and suddenly that it left us all shocked. You did not get time to make preparations for the Hereafter. But your departure made us realise that we should start making arrangements. Who knows when his or her turn will be next?

A few days back an acquaintance of ours suddenly died in a road accident. He had gone to Pakistan for a week to attend the wedding of his cousin. He died on the very day when he was scheduled to return to England. He was only 28 years old. He was buried in Pakistan and he left behind a young wife and a two-year-old son. It is absolutely true that we do not know where, when and how we will die. It is all in Allah's (SWT) control. It often happens that people go to Pakistan or some other country for holidays and die there and are sometimes buried abroad. Some people live their whole life in their own country and travel once to visit their children or siblings and die there. There are so many such examples around us, but still we do not prepare for it. Why is this so? Adam, what is it which prevents us from preparing?

I sometimes feel that all the following things act as hurdles in our preparation like: children, money, house, selfishness, our ego, love for this world and our desires.

Adam, a friend's father died. I went to see her. She told me that her father was offering Salah when he died. He bowed in prostration, but did not get up again. Praise be to Allah (SWT), what a beautiful Shahadah and what a superior activity he was engaged in at the time of his death. When angels had come to take away his soul, they would have found him in an exalting posture, Masha'Allah. Adam I also wish for such a respectable death. May Allah (SWT) enable me to recite the Kalimah and may the Angel of death find me prostrated before Allah (SWT) when he comes to take me, Ameen.

When we come across such examples we never think that this can happen to us. Our general notion is that these things pertain to other people. We have got plenty of time to make preparations. If not today, no worries, we will do it tomorrow, or the day after or next week, then next month or next year. Thus we keep on postponing this year after year, and put off even more planning like *Sheikh Chilli* (a popular character in Urdu literature who lives in dream-land and makes endless plans), till Allah's (SWT) summon comes and we still have no preparations made.

Adam, suppose I have to go to Pakistan and I postpone my packing daily, thinking that I will do it the next day. Finally, the day of my flight arrives and the departure time approaches. If I have not prepared, I will have to leave for Pakistan without any of my essential belongings. What would be my feeling at such a time? I will blame myself for wasting my time in other things and neglecting my packing. I would think of myself as a very stupid person.

Similarly we will prove ourselves to be really stupid if we go to Allah (SWT) with our handbag of good deeds empty. We will not have anything of benefit to our credit. Adam, preparations must always be made beforehand. If the time passes, then nothing is left except anguish and gloom.

That is why Allah (SWT) says in the holy Quran:

"And this life of the world is nothing but amusement and play. And undoubtedly the home of the Hereafter, indeed that is the true life. If only they knew"

Surah Al-Ankabut (The Spider), 29:64

And:

"Rivalry for piling up [wealth] has kept you heedless till you saw your graves."

Surah At-Takaathur (Piling up), 102:1-2

As a poet said:

No one knows [the time] of his death
Though we collect things to last a hundred years, but do not know what the next moment holds.

Adam, I love this prayer which Allah (SWT) has taught us through Quran.

رَبَّنَا آتِنَا فِي الدُّنْيَا حَسَنَةً وَفِي الآخِرَةِ حَسَنَةً وَقِنَا عَذَابَ النَّارِ

"O our lord grant us good in this world and also good in the Hereafter and save us from the torment of hellfire."

Surah Al-Baqarah (The Cow), 2:201

Adam, I offer this prayer for the entire Muslim Ummah. May Allah (SWT) guide us, save us from the humiliation of this world and Hereafter and may He save us from the torture of hell, Ameen.

May you be in Allah's protection, my child.

Your Mother,
Urfana Ayub

Letter No 6.

The right path

My dear son, Adam.
Peace be upon you.

I hope that you will be peaceful and content in Allah's (SWT) protection. Your journey in this finite world ended so quickly. You may not even imagine what is happening in this world seven years on.

On one hand evil is spreading. We see wrong acts being done everywhere. The evil has spread to such an extent that it is no longer considered as wrong or sinful. On the other hand Islam is spreading at a fast rate Masha'Allah.

If there is darkness from sins and vices on one side, the other side is ablaze with the radiance of Islam and Imaan (faith). But people are engulfed by the darkness of the sins which does not let them see. Just like a man travelling on a road at night will not be able find his way, these people are wandering about aimlessly. The ones who have got Imaan and Allah's (SWT) radiance can distinctly see the path they have to tread upon. Many people are now blessed with the blessing of Imaan who did not even believe in Islam before. These are the people who have recently converted to Islam, and Allah (SWT) has filled their hearts with the radiance of Imaan, Masha'Allah. Adam, these people inspire me.

We were born in Muslim families. We inherited Islam from our ancestors. That is why we do not value it. We do not have to make any sacrifices for it, so we have come to take it for granted. We feel at liberty to treat it as we desire. We act on Islam when we feel like; we offer Salah if we find time. In short, we have modified our religion according to our whim and ease. But the people who convert to Islam by choice have to make lots of sacrifices for it. They abandon their religion, their parents and their love, their friends and their world for Allah's (SWT) sake. They go through an extremely difficult time and they need a lot of integrity and resilience to remain on their chosen path. One feels very happy to meet these people. Now such people are my companions in religion. Many renowned scholars, who belonged to different religions before, have converted to Islam and are working as preachers of our religion. All such people have made efforts to understand Islam. So instead of the veteran Muslims teaching, these new converts, Praise be to Allah, are now teaching Islam to us.

That is why it is said, *"Allah (SWT) gives guidance to whom He wills and leads astray whom He wills".* I did not understand its wisdom before, but now I know that whoever is really desirous of true guidance, Allah (SWT) will guide him/her. But anyone who wants to go astray, Allah (SWT) will let them wander because Allah (SWT) is very well aware of what goes on in our hearts and minds! People often do not understand this and Nauzobillah (Allah forbid) blame Allah (SWT) for their misguidance, saying *"Had Allah (SWT) willed, He would surely have led us towards the right path. What can we do, if Allah (SWT) did not guide us?"* And thus they absolve themselves of all responsibility.

Adam, nowadays most people's situations can be described by this poem:

My tongue became silent as I was about to utter something
I hesitated calling myself a Muslim
It is not that I do not believe in Allah (SWT)
But I was kind of afraid calling myself a believer
I could not bring myself to offer even a single Salah
And the prayer caller's voice finally died away
When a non-believer inquired me what month it was
Water dropped from my hands as I was about to
say"Ramadhan"
When somebody asked me about the dust laden book in my
cupboard
I got buried with shame before I could utter "Quran"
After this he became quiet
As if he had stopped himself from calling me an animal

May Allah (SWT) protect us all and may He keep us on the right path with firm conviction, Ameen. Allah (SWT) has made man the best of His creations. I pray that Allah (SWT) keeps us so and prevent us from falling to the level of animals who can only eat, drink and propagate their species with no understanding of why they were created. Alas, today this earth has far more people than true believers.

May Allah (SWT) be your Guardian.

Your Mother,
Urfana Ayub

Letter No 7.

Realising the value of time

My dear child, Adam.
Peace be upon you.

Loads of love and prayers for you Adam. I often get irritated at certain things; those things which were stressed upon as part of my upbringing and have now become a part of me. I get annoyed when people go against these principles. Today, I faced one such situation. Forgive me Adam, when I talk to you as if you are still in our house and you know what is going on. My dear son, I forget sometimes that you no longer live in our house. You have your own new house where we are all destined to go one day.

Well, as I was saying Adam, I don't understand why people neglect punctuality. For example, if a person is invited to someone's place at 1pm, why does he prefer turning up at 2pm? Why don't people arrive at the specified time? I feel we don't give two hoots to the time. Time in itself is very precious. It is more precious than money, but people do not understand it. Why? People who waste time, in reality, are themselves being wasted by time. Such people are often left empty-handed without any success in worldly or religious matters or the Hereafter.

At times this insensitivity of people depresses me. They don't realise what they are doing is wrong. They do not even perceive their mistake as a mistake. Probably when an error or fault spreads in the community to such an extent that people begin to accept it, then it no longer remains a mistake in their eyes.

Often, if you happen to arrive at an occasion or a ceremony on time, apart from a few people, there is nobody present. I understand that one may get inadvertently delayed in reaching somewhere, as everyone has their own commitments, and sometimes there is a genuine reason for the delay. But if this attitude becomes a custom, then to me it is more of an excuse than a valid reason.

We are clever people, Adam! If we do not intend to do something on time, we conjure up many reasons for it. I call these lame excuses and not reasons! If we really want to do something, we get it done five minutes in advance. But if we have decided not to do it, then we put forward lots of excuses and limitations and shy away from the responsibility. While doing this, we never realise that our Creator and Sustainer is aware of all the open and hidden secrets of our heart. We can betray the people but never Allah (SWT).

Our beloved Prophet (PBUH) said:

"Consider the former five things as an opportunity before the latter five things:

1.   *Health before sickness*
2.   *Youth before old age*
3.   *Leisure before involvement*
4.   *Richness before poverty*
5.   *Life before death."*

(Tirmidhi)

Adam, I have begun to value time more after you. During my childhood, since there was a military atmosphere in our house, we were used to getting things done on a set timetable. But after your loss, I felt a new value for time. Maybe it is because I could not hold your last moments in this world. Not half a day, or a few hours or a few seconds. No, I could not even hold a single moment. It was then that I realised that time is more precious than money.

We can buy anything on earth with money except time. Time is more powerful than money. Generally we are very cautious in spending money, but are more liberal in wasting time. We need to change our attitudes. Time demands respect. We have to value time. History has been a witness to the examples where Allah (SWT) granted success to the people who valued time.

The Hereafter is like an ocean and this world is just a drop of water in the ocean in comparison. All our tests are related to this drop only which we are bent upon wasting without thinking. We must ask Allah (SWT) to grant blessing (Barakah) in our time. We should spend our time in those things which will benefit us in the Hereafter. Try to excel in good deeds. If you get a chance to help someone, do not let go of it. Time is more precious than gold, silver or diamonds. So realise its importance and spend it in the best possible way, like making supplications while doing your daily chores and remembering Allah (SWT) by reciting His name or praising Him.

Hadrat Abu Bakr (RA) used to supplicate like this, "*Oh Allah (SWT) please do not keep us in darkness and do not make us oblivious of the time."* He further used to say *"Please grant magnitude to my time"*, Ameen.

Our beloved Prophet (PBUH) said,

"There are two of Allah's (SWT) bounties from which people do not benefit as they should: health and leisure."

(Bukhari)

Adam, I feel that we are all under the misconception that we will never fall ill, nor will we ever become dependent on others. In other words, we will never face a situation where we will not find the chance to pray and supplicate. Similarly, leisure is also a blessing of Allah (SWT) which people often forget will end one day. Time and circumstances completely change one's life. We must utilise the time which we have at our hands today in the best possible way.

We can also get an idea about the importance of time from the fact that Allah (SWT) has mentioned time in two Surahs of the Quran, *Surah Al-Asr* (The Time) and *Surah Ad Dahr* (The Era).

Somebody asked Luqman Hakeem (Aesop) *"Where did you learn wisdom from?"* He replied, *"From fools"*. Adam, we must all pay attention to our speech. We waste a lot of time in useless gossip. We must try to recite Allah's (SWT) praise during all of our free time.

Adam, previously I thought that prayer was only possible on a prayer mat. But now I know that we can indulge in prayer even while doing our daily jobs like walking, washing dishes,

44

cooking food, driving a car, ironing clothes etc. In fact, we can remember and praise our Creator at all times. Every minute is precious. We can earn great rewards from Allah (SWT) in these moments. Performing Wudhu (ablution) is not mandatory for Allah's (SWT) praise and remembrance. Yet it is said that when man is involved in Allah's (SWT) remembrance (Zikr), the angels are busy building a house for him in heaven. As soon as he abandons the Zikr, the angels also halt the work they were doing. No form of prayer is easier then Zikr.

In today's world the major cause of time wasting is technology. Where it has provided many benefits to mankind, it also brings many drawbacks especially for those people who have no definite aim in life. A man with a purpose in life would not like to waste hours and hours on telephone conversation. Similarly such a person would not be a slave of Facebook, Twitter, WhatsApp, Viber and the internet. A true believer is only Allah's (SWT) slave. But these satanic inventions have left no stone unturned to mislead mankind and waste their time.

Allah (SWT) has taught the best time management to man by giving us the five Salah. Each Salah has a time period stipulated for it which helps us to understand the value of time. Allah (SWT) has taught us multiple ways by which we can utilise our time to full advantage and thus gain access to Heaven.

"Reciting Subhan Allahi Wa Bi Hamdihi (Allah is free from imperfection and His is the praise) 100 times a day will purge man of all his sins, even if they were equal to the surf on the oceans in number."

(Bukhari)

Adam, unless man has set an objective in life, he cannot utilise his time in a positive and productive manner. It is necessary for us to be strict with ourselves. We must set new goals before us and then make all efforts to achieve these goals; just like students toil hard to get a degree because they see their goal in it. An academic degree is a benefit for the students because it will help them secure a good job and salary. Similarly, we as Muslims have to fashion a new way for our lives and time which will help us to reach our destination.

There is another superb way of spending our time and that is involvement in Dua (supplication). Supplication is prayer. Indulging in supplication is one hundred percent to our advantage. One can be occupied in worship at all times. In the same manner, meditating on this universe is also a form of prayer which allows us to get closer to Allah (SWT).

Adam, we must remember that our life is not meant for petty jobs. We have to carry out our own assessment and contemplate which of our actions will benefit us most in the Hereafter. Then spend our time, money and energy to attain that specific goal!

Adam it is my heartfelt prayer that Allah (SWT) may grant us an expanse of time, so that we can perform good deeds in our available moments and hours and let these good deeds be our tools to get into Heaven, Ameen.

May you be in Allah's (SWT) protection my son.

Your Mother, Urfana Ayub

Letter No 8.

Moaning nullifies the gratitude and gratitude nullifies moaning

Adam, my child, Peace be upon you.
Love and prayers for you.

How are you? I was anxious to share some things with you. Yesterday, I attended an Islamic lecture where I learnt the following things. Why has Allah (SWT) given us this heart? What is its purpose? Who must dwell in it? How to take care of it? Who actually lives in there?

Adam, Allah (SWT) has given this heart to us so that we may inhabit it with Allah (SWT) and be filled with His love and remembrance. But do you know who lives there in reality? Our hearts are filled by this world: our relatives, our friends, glamour, money, possessions, vanity, as well as jealousy, envy and love for life. Look how many things are residing in our hearts. There is no space left for Allah (SWT) and His love. Our hearts will not find solace and comfort until we make enough room in it for Allah (SWT) who is the Master of our hearts and also its rightful owner. I pray to Allah (SWT).

As the poet said:

> *O Lord grant such a desire to hearts of the Muslim*
> *Which will energise their heart and stimulate the soul*

> **(Allama Iqbal)**

The main reason for our anxieties and apprehensions is that we do not give due rights to those who deserve it. When we do not give due rights to their rightful owners, we will be considered as oppressors. We are running after this world and its love. Though we are exhausted by this chase, still we haven't got enough of it. From morning till night all our endeavours are directed towards attaining this world only. We have forgotten that in this process we have lost our five Salahs of the day. We have never opened the Quran and we have let go of all the opportunities of performing good deeds even if they came our way. In short we are following our hearts blindly.

Allah (SWT) says in the Quran:

"Say 'If it be that your fathers, your sons, your brothers, your wives, or your kindred; the wealth that you have gained; the commerce in which you fear a decline or the dwellings in which you delight, are dearer to you than Allah, or His Messenger, or the striving in His cause; then wait until Allah brings about His decision, and Allah guides not the rebellious'."

Surah At-Taubah (The Repentance), 9:24

Jihad does not only imply fighting your enemies with a sword in the battlefield. It has a much wider spectrum, which is being steadfast on Islam and fighting against the evil of our mind and spirit, against social malpractices and to raise a voice against the injustices done for the love of blood. We are well aware of our disobedience to Allah (SWT), and after pleasing our souls, after doing everything that our hearts desire, we put all the blame on Satan and try to act innocent as if nothing was in our power.

As a poet said:

I feel like laughing on "Mr. Man"
Who sins by his will and blames the Satan

We tend to forget that Allah (SWT) has made man the best of His creations. We are the Ummah (followers) of our last Prophet Muhammad (PBUH). Allah (SWT) made us Muslims. He could have made us birds, insects, buffaloes, elephants or even ants, Praise be to Allah (SWT). Allah (SWT) made us his most superior creation, but we have forgotten everything. We have forgotten to give Allah (SWT) His rights. We don't know what thankfulness is. Our woes and complaints never end.

They say that if we do not thank Allah (SWT); if our heads do not bow in gratitude on all the bounties that He has showered on us, then we have no right to cry when grief befalls us, or to dare complain to Allah (SWT) about it.

The Sustainer has said "*I will grant more to him who is thankful to Me.*" Thankfulness makes us closer to our Creator. It nurtures humility in man. I feel Adam that those people who are grateful to Allah (SWT) are also thankful to their fellow beings. There are some people who manage to express gratitude to Allah (SWT), but they feel small and belittled if they need to thank others.

A few days back Adam, I heard a heart-touching sermon. May Allah (SWT) make this a source of permanent reward for the person who delivered it, Ameen. He talked about two contrasting qualities of gratitude and reproach. He said that "*gratitude dies away with reproach and reproach kills*

49

gratitude." Now it is up to us humans which of these two qualities we choose for ourselves. If our balance tilts toward gratitude, then Allah (SWT) will enhance our bounties and make them lasting. We cannot restrain the bounties and blessings of Allah (SWT) by chains, but we can make them last by gratitude.

Allah (SWT) is most benevolent and ever forgiving. He showers mankind with His blessings all the time. We need to think deeply and meditate in order to recognise the millions of blessings present all around us, and then we need to thank Allah (SWT) for it. The more we acknowledge and praise Allah (SWT) for the blessings, the more they will last and remain with us. For example, the blessings of our human organs, our hands, feet, eyes, heart, brain and a healthy body etc.

In order to adopt the quality of gratitude and to avoid thanklessness, our beloved Prophet (PBUH) has given the best advice: *"Keep those people in mind who have less than you in terms of money and worldly status"*, and the feeling of gratitude will surge in you. Do not look at those who have been given more than you when it comes to money and worldly things lest the blessings which have been granted to you today may become small and insignificant in your eyes and the feeling of reproach emerges in your hearts.

Yet humans cannot help complaining. We indulge in moaning and whining all the time, even in our happy moments. We cannot seem to refrain from alluding to our complaints either openly or subtly. The more we whine, the more our troubles will zoom in close to us and sometimes become our destiny.

As Allah (SWT) says in the glorious Quran:

"And surely We have established you in the earth and there appointed for you livelihood; little thanks you show."

Surah Al-A'raf (The Heights), 7:10

I have learned that I have the power to decide whether I need Allah's (SWT) blessings or not. Do I wish to enhance these blessings? If the answer is *"yes"*, then I need to be grateful to Allah (SWT) and His creations. Remember this gratitude can only be attained by completely eliminating our protests and complaints. So when I remove all complaints from my heart consciously, and at the same time keep myself engaged in deep thinking and meditation, only then will I be able to thank Allah (SWT) in a befitting manner.

Adam, ever since you went away, I have never complained to Allah (SWT). I have always been grateful to Him. Maybe that is the reason He showered perseverance on me. Otherwise I would not have the courage or strength to bear this grief.

I pray with all my heart that may Allah (SWT) remove the trait of complaining from our hearts and introduce one of gratitude instead, Ameen. I am thankful to Allah (SWT) with my every breath that he made you my son in this brief worldly life. Praise be to Allah I taught you to walk by holding your finger, and now that you are no more I am sailing though the ocean of my dreams holding your finger, engulfed by the fragrance of your being. I am also a traveller along the same path which you are treading. I know these paths are destined by Allah (SWT). You were just an excuse to put me on my right track. This journey is opening and enlightening my whole being praise be to Allah (SWT).

Thank you my beloved Adam. Allah Hafiz.

Your Mother,
Urfana Ayub

Letter No 9.

The New Path

Dear son Adam.
Lots of prayers for my child.

We are all fine and miss you a lot. Time is passing quickly. No one can control its speed. No matter how successful man is, he is helpless before time. He cannot move even a single moment forward or backward. No doubt everything is in the control of Allah (SWT). Nobody can lift a finger nor can any leaf fall from a tree without the permission of our Creator. We are powerless. The absolute sovereignty lies with Allah (SWT). He can do whatever He wishes and whenever He wishes. He only has to say *"Kun"* (be done) and the thing gets done. There is wisdom in every decision of His, but we, with our limited knowledge, cannot fathom that wisdom. He gives us opportunities to get close to Him by putting us through different tests and losses, but most people do not understand it. The paths which my life led me to after you, Adam, and all the people who became part of my life are all Allah's (SWT) wisdom. I ask for His guidance at every step of my life so that I can clearly see His wisdom and the right path.

A New Path

The path which I found after you
The path which I had never thought of, the one you showed
me
I look for you at every step on this path

Knowing very well that you won't be or nor will be there
But my heart is filled with your memories
And my eyes are tearful in remembering you
Don't know where that time has gone in which you were alive
Don't know where those moments have gone in which you
used to laugh
Now I only have this world in which you no longer live
But I have a heart in which you dwell
You are alive in the world of my mind
You still laugh in the world of my heart
Your departure left me at a strange turn in life
A turn which I had never even thought of before
This new turn is my companion now
I have found escorts on this new path
After you I have found many friends on this new path
May Allah (SWT) protect all my friends
May Allah (SWT) bless all my friends, Ameen

(Urfana Ayub)

It is a fact that *Taray Janay Kay Baad* connected me with Allah (SWT), with a lot of people and their sorrows, and above all it connected me with myself. To connect people with their own selves is one of the greatest favours of Allah (SWT) to make people realise the many different ways in which Allah (SWT) has blessed them. Yet people neither consider these blessings of Allah (SWT) nor thank Him.

Adam, I realised after you how beautiful the sky is. I began to see the flying birds. I developed the ability to sense the different seasons of Summer, Autumn, Winter and Spring. I found new pleasure in the blooming of flowers, the shedding of leaves, the heat of summers and chill of winters, Praise be to Allah (SWT).

Adam there is so much attraction and appeal in every creation of Allah (SWT). But alas we are so much engrossed in man-made things that we do not pay enough attention to Allah's (SWT) creation. New technology easily impresses us, but when eating fruit we never think how Allah (SWT) has made each fruit a different colour, appearance and taste, even though the plants are all were irrigated by the same water.

Allah (SWT) says in the holy Quran:

"It is He who sends down rain from the sky; from it is drink and from it is foliage in which you pasture [animal]. With which He causes to grow for you the crops and Olives, Palm trees, Grapevines, and fruits of every kind for you. Indeed in it is a sign for the people who ponder."

Surah An-Nahl (The Bees), 16:10-11

I too never thought of this fact before while eating fruit like Pomegranates, but now I am amazed when I realise that we cannot even count the seeds in it. There are so many different sections. Allah (SWT) preserved all of them. Each seed is of a slightly different shape, but how superbly they are arranged in the fruit without wasting any space and how unique is their taste and nutrition Masha'Allah. Then there are flowers! You know, Adam, how much I've always liked flowers. Now I try to perceive their colour, design and fragrance. I am totally overawed by them. I cannot understand Allah's (SWT) Magnificence and Majesty. His every decision is perfect, His every action precise. Every creation of Allah (SWT) invites us to think and meditate.

Allah (SWT) says in the Quran:

"If you wish to count Allah's (SWT) blessings you will not be able to calculate. Assuredly Allah is oft-forgiving, most merciful."

Surah An-Nahl (The Bees), 16:18

The fact is, that it is only the person who has real sight who tries to recognise Allah (SWT) by His creations and acts according to His instructions. Otherwise, he is blind despite having two eyes.

Previously Adam, I only saw this world, people and things. After you went away I have begun to ponder and contemplate over them and it has left me with a strange and pleasant feeling, as if someone has woken me up from deep sleep. Which type of world was I living in before?

May you be in Allah's (SWT) protection my child.
With lots of love and prayers.

Your Mother
Urfana Ayub

He would not leave

Dear son Adam,
Lots of prayers for you.

Do you remember I used to love colours? I like them even today. Colours make life beautiful. They have an aura of their own. Every colour is unique. Sometimes people associate different colours with different sentiments. I like using all the colours even now. When we wear a new colour, I feel that particular colour has a whole world attached to it. Adam, I enjoy working with colour, whether watercolours, canvas painting, screen printing or fabric printing.

I am terrified of how a person who cannot see this world would feel; whose world is dark and who cannot appreciate the colours spread around him. The only colour in their world is black, with no light. This makes me think of the grave. The darkness and confines of the grave paralyse me with fear. What can a blind person see? He cannot recognise any colour. He doesn't even know what different colours look like. All the colours are the same for him.

Adam I have never adequately thanked my Lord for blessing me with two eyes with which I see this world.

These questions often arise in my mind, Adam:

Why are we humans like this?

Are we insensitive?
Are we also blind?

Apparently we have eyes but we lack insight. We are able to see many things with our eyes, but many things can only be perceived through inner sight. I have started realising this. I am a lucky and blessed woman because I have got two eyes and I can see with them both.

A few days back, Adam, a car, probably a taxi, was travelling directly in front of my car. The traffic was heavy due to schools home time. I could clearly see the driver of the car in front of me. He had one eye only. In place of his other eye, there was just a flap of skin. There were no eyebrows or eyelashes either.

Maybe that eye was damaged in an accident or surgery, or maybe it was like that from birth. I don't know, but his face scared me. I immediately thanked Allah (SWT) for granting me two eyes, praise be to Allah. These two eyes on our face are more precious than the riches of the whole world. Adam, I consider myself to be a very lucky woman whom Allah (SWT) has blessed with two hands and two feet. I have seen many people in wheelchairs with amputated legs. Some people do not have arms or hands. I thank Allah (SWT) for granting me healthy limbs, praise be to Allah. My ability to walk is more precious than the riches of this whole world, praise be to Allah (SWT).

When I take Ahmad to school in the morning, I often see a teenage boy walking on the footpath. His face is turned upward toward the sky. The movement of his limbs and his facial expression indicate that he has a disability. Whenever

I see him, I thank Allah (swt) for having blessed me with a healthy body and mind.

I few days back I went with Dadi Ammi to meet one of her friends. I met the friend's daughter there, all of whose children had mental disabilities. An acquaintances of ours has two tall and handsome sons, but both are mentally disabled also. Wherever I go, I am introduced as *"Adam's mother"*. When I saw those children, I thanked Allah (swt) for granting me with healthy offspring.

We humans are thankless creatures. If a couple is childless, they will regret it throughout their lives. They will never realise that maybe Allah (swt) has granted them with another blessing like good health instead. If a husband is not considerate, but the children are very good in all aspects, the wife will keep on wishing for a better husband. She does not understand that Allah (swt) has granted her obedient children as an alternative for a good husband. If a man has a good home and loving relations, but he does not have a decent job, he will keep on wishing for a better job only.

Adam, I sometimes think that we do not understand Allah's (swt) Hikamah (wisdom). If he keeps a person deficient in a certain blessing, He grants him another bounty in abundance instead. We must understand this if we want to live a content life, otherwise our hearts will remain restless. Why do we always want a good husband instead of a bad one, perfect children, a decent job and a large house? There is no other solution for us! How would such a person come to terms with life?

After you Adam, I ponder: what has Allah (swt) given me by

taking you back and making me a mother of three children instead of four? How has He made up for the loss of my fourth child? Allah (SWT) enlightened my heart. I did not seek a fourth child to replace you, because I knew that a son was not necessary to make up for the lack of a son. But what did I gain instead? What was Allah's (SWT) wisdom?

After you Adam, Allah (SWT) brought us and our whole family closer to Him. We began to fear Allah's (SWT) wrath. We became aware of our preparation for the Hereafter and of the grave. We learned to thank Him for all His blessings. He made us firm in our conviction and He made us believe in His wisdom. He gave us tears, tender hearts, valued relationships and love and sincerity in our dealings with each other.

Due to the grace and benevolence of Allah (SWT), *Taray Janay Kay Baad* came into existence. This book connected me with the sorrow of other people. Allah (SWT) endowed me with feelings for others and made me eager to participate in good deeds Masha'Allah. He enabled me to contribute to charitable causes through those works which would be a source of permanent reward for you, praise be to Allah.

Your loss became a means for us to prepare for the Hereafter. Otherwise, we would have kept on living as before until our lives ended. For me the grief of your departure is Allah's wisdom and decision. I accept this decision with all my heart because death is our destiny too. You are still here with us even after death. Indeed you are ahead of us all in doing good deeds. The fact is, Adam, that you are still very much alive in our hearts.

He would not leave

The person who dwelt in my eyes always
How I tried to forget him but he would not leave
I tried to meet him in my dreams but could not
He is beyond my dreams but from my heart he would not leave
He came to reside in my heart but could not stay
He was not destined to stay, but from my heart he would not leave
How I wanted him to leave my heart
But he has came back to stay
Despite all my efforts he lives in my heart
All my efforts went in vain and he would not leave
I will let him stay in my heart forever
Because I know I can never make him go

(Urfana Ayub)

I am missing you Adam. My heart is mournful. It is a long time since I saw you in my dreams. I often pray to see you in my dreams. Though this meeting is short-lived, it is still very beautiful. I pray to Allah (SWT) that may He make me meet you soon. I am waiting for you in my dream world.

I give you in Allah's (SWT) protection, my child. Allah Hafiz.

Your Mother,
Urfana Ayub

61

Letter No 11.

Fragile relationships

Dear son, my child Adam Ayub, peace be upon you
Lots of love and prayers for you.

I am trying to recall how I started writing *Taray Janay
Kay Baad*. No doubt it was with Allah's (SWT) help and
blessing. And after that it was you who made me write it!
I had never thought that I would write a book in my life.
People appreciated *Taray Janay Kay Baad* very much and
encourgaed me to write again. I received hundreds of
emails, letters and telephone calls from people in which
they provided me with their feedback.

Many times I tried to write, but could not. Maybe Allah (SWT)
did not want me to. Now, five years after you left us, Allah
(SWT) has made me write once again. The reason for writing
is again you. Adam, even today you are walking with
me, holding onto my hand or maybe I am holding onto
your hand. You are present at every turn of my life.
The perception that you are still here even after your
going away is very strong in me. It is not only due to
the fact that you are alive in my heart at all times, but
like a living person, you are very much involved in the
good deeds being done in the world today. You are being
talked about. People remember you by name and mention
you.

There are many people who never saw you when you were
alive, but know you now. Masha'Allah you are loved even

today. Many people's prayers are with you. May Allah (SWT) accept all these prayers in your favour, Ameen.

Love is such a unique perception, Adam. Just like a fragrance, or a flower which makes this world beautiful. The highest and most superior of all these affections is the one for Allah (SWT) and His last Prophet Muhammad (PBUH). After that comes love for parents and children. But there is no doubt that a mother's love is beyond compare.

As a poet said:

> *I am lucky my mother is alive*
> *Angels are praying for me all the time*

Prayers can be truly magical. There is magic in a parent's prayers. They are so sincere and intense that Allah (SWT) accepts them. Allah (SWT) is aware of the honesty of our hearts. He knows how strongly and sincerely we supplicate to Him. Allah's (SWT) bounties are limitless. There is no shortage or deficiency in them. The fault lies within our prayers, our faith and our trust in Allah (SWT). I am lucky to have the blessings of both my parents. May Allah (SWT) grant long life to them both, Ameen.

Adam, we do not give enough importance to our loved ones. We are under the impression that they will stay with us forever. We do not value them, and when they go away suddenly our homes and hearts are left empty. I have always valued my relationships. Nana Abba and Nani Ammi always stressed the importance of relationships in our lives. They taught me to value, love and respect them. This care for relationships intensified in me after your departure. I realise how precious relationships are. More delicate than glass, they will break if we do not nurture them and the cracks will be clearly visible.

Relationships are invaluable. Allah (SWT) has emphasised the need to maintain and safeguard them, especially our relationships with our parents, as mentioned several times in the Quran. But other relationships too must be respected.

Today our society has become very selfish. We have ignored the sanctity of those relationships whose respect and regard is compulsory. We have started expecting favours from all those relationships which are binding. We want to benefit from every relationship, but do not want to give anything in return.

This world, its people and relationships; all have become selfish. Love has been replaced by hatred. Restlessness has replaced peace. Homes have become loveless. People have forgotten to smile, to compliment and thank others. Satan is successful in his endeavors yet people are oblivious to him.

These things distress me, Adam. When I see the lives of people around me engulfed in the vicious cycle of anxiety, I want to tell them to stop and think for a few minutes. How can they find solace and serenity if they keep breaking others' hearts to achieve worldly gains? When we make people sad, Allah (SWT) is not happy with us. Our beloved Prophet (PBUH) said:

"He who severs links with blood relatives will not enter

paradise"

Narrated in Bukhari, Kitab ul Adab (Book on Manners/ General Behaviour) 5984.

Maybe people think that teasing others and causing grief to them is not a great sin. One only needs to keep Allah (SWT) pleased. They forget that Allah's (SWT) benevolence is very vast. He can forgive you, if you repent sincerely and ask for His forgiveness. But making other people happy is a hard task, especially if you have caused them pain.

As a poet said:

*Only the feeling of guilt, prostration and tears in the eyes.
How easy it is to please you O Allah (SWT)*

Our relationships with other people are more fragile in nature. After you Adam, I sometimes apologise to other people on your behalf. I ask them to forgive you, if knowingly or unknowingly you broke their heart or were unjust to them in any way.

Adam, sometimes we do not hurt others consciously, but heedlessly or due to some misunderstanding, or simply stupidly we do something which is painful for them. Under such circumstances we must apologise to others. It is better to ask for forgiveness of people here in this world rather than in the hereafter, when the entire human race will be assembled before Allah (SWT).

The problem is, we feel embarrassed to apologise in front of a few people as if this will lower our self-esteem. But we forget that in the hereafter, when every human being is gathered before our Creator, won't we feel embarrassed then? Won't we feel disgraced then? The insult of that day will be much greater in magnitude than this world's shame. If only we respect our relationships! If only we act on those principles which have been laid down by our religion to guide us so that we may enjoy our relationships with love and esteem.

The glorious Quran states:

"Fear Allah (SWT) in Whose name you ask for (your rights) and pay attention to the ties of relationship/kinship".

Surah An-Nisa' (The Women), 4:1

Once someone gave me very good advice. *"Be selfless and sincere with others. Respect and love them so much that you do not need to remind them to pray for you as people often ask. Try to become such a person for whom others supplicate on their own without being asked to do so."*

I pray to Allah (SWT) that may He make me such a person who maintains relations with other people only to please Him. Let other people be happy with me for Allah's (SWT) sake. Let me love other people for Allah's (SWT) sake and let me hate them for His sake as well, Ameen.

I am very fond of our Prophet's (PBUH) prayer, *"O Lord I ask You for Your love, I ask for the love of that person who loves You. Let me do such deeds which bring me closer to You".*

(Tirmidhi)

I leave you in Allah's (SWT) protection.

Your Mother,
Urfana Ayub

Letter No 12.

Dreams do sometimes come true

Dear son, Adam Ayub.
Lots of love and duas.

I am very upset today. Not for you, but for someone else. I am acutely aware of the fact that man is very powerless. Nothing is in our control. No matter how rich, famous, educated or in charge of things we seem to be, in reality we are nothing and all these worldly medals do not mean anything either. If any one of our body parts stops functioning, we do not have the capability to change it. When Allah (SWT) wants to put someone to a test, he takes something away from him suddenly.

May Allah (SWT) protect us from all trials, Ameen. No matter how religious we are, any such test is also a test of our faith. That is why older people used to say, *"One may lose money but not Imaan (faith)"*. Because when someone loses money, or it is stolen from them, that person would have suspicions and he may start blaming someone for theft without any proof. This suspicion can ultimately lead to sin. Faith is the most precious of all possessions.

These days one of my friends is also passing through a difficult time. I have advised her to safeguard her faith in her situation. Insha 'Allah, Allah (SWT) will ease her situation. If we protect our Imaan from outside influences, Insha 'Allah it will prosper. But if we lose our faith in difficult circumstances, the danger is, we may never regain it. The level of faith keeps increasing and decreasing. We must always keep a watch over it.

Today when I heard of my friend's circumstances, my heart and my eyes cried. Adam, now I find comfort in crying. This association with tears is also because of you and it has strengthened my relationship with Allah (SWT).

As a poet said:

Do not try to save your mirror from breaking, as your mirror is the one
which when broken becomes more precious in the eyes of its maker
In this case mirror means human heart.

Adam, do you know Allah (SWT) is my best friend now. Previously I used to talk to Allah (SWT) and you and your siblings used to ask me who I was talking to. I still talk to Him, but silently, in my heart, and He answers me. This is such a beautiful and exquisite relationship that I cannot even describe but can only feel. I have named this relationship *"magic"*.

One example is that on 7th May 2012 you turned 21. Masha'Allah, in my imagination you were a handsome young man. All the family members gathered and remembered you. I was acutely conscious of the fact that, had you been alive, you would have completed your education this year.

Like other parents I also wanted to get your degree framed and displayed on a wall, but being more practical, I knew this was not possible.

But then something magical happened. A few voice messages had collected on the landline phone. Once I have heard them I have a habit of deleting them. Most are usually promotional messages from various companies for the sale of their products. But today there was something different amongst the messages:

"This message is for the parents of Adam Ayub. We are from the Graduation Department of Leeds University. We are fully aware that, had Adam Ayub been alive today, he would have been awarded his degree this year. We would like you to contact us on this number....."

This was a miracle Adam! Allah (SWT) was answering all the unsaid queries and desires of my heart. After listening to this message, for a long time I stood still with tears flowing incessantly down my face. I listened to the message repeatedly and thought maybe I was not hearing it properly or maybe it was all a dream!

When I contacted the university they invited us formally to the graduation ceremony where they would be giving Adam his posthumous degree. They also sought our permission to issue a special award in your name, the "Adam Ayub Award". I was told this award would be given to a student on your course who feels that you contributed to his success and encouraged him when you were studying with him in the university.

I was stunned at Allah's (SWT) power. No doubt it was my Lord's grace and benevolence praise be to Allah .
As a poet said:

There must be someone managing this universe - that is Allah (SWT)
He who cannot be seen but is evident everywhere - that is Allah (SWT)

He has vision, He can hear, He even knows what goes on in our hearts He who is enlightening our unconscious - that is Allah (SWT)

Do not search for Him in idols, look for Him in changing seasons

He who is turning day into night and night into day - that is Allah (SWT)

(Muzaffar Warsi)

26th July 2012 was an unforgettable day for us, which gave us many new memories. This was the day your brother Arslan was going to receive your degree on the stage on your behalf. When he came to me dressed up and ready for the occasion, my eyes wanted to see you there. My heart was grieving and tears did not stop flowing from my eyes. Masha'Allah Arslan was looking very handsome in his new grey suit.

We received a lot of respect at the University. Front row seats were reserved for us. They issued extra passes which allowed the whole family, including Baba and Phuphie, to attend your graduation ceremony. We were all involved in your celebration with mixed emotions of happiness and sorrow.

This day made me extremely proud, but at the same time my head also bowed before Allah (SWT) in thankfulness. When Arslan walked on the stage to receive your degree the entire hall resonated with the words, *"Adam Ayub Posthumous Award"*. I could not stop my tears for even a moment in this gathering and clapping of people. I cannot put down my feelings of that moment on paper. Only my Creator and a mother's heart knew what I went through.

On that day the Adam Ayub Award was handed over by me to your classmate Craig Hammond. He told me that your smile was an inspiration for him. He was shy of speaking publicly and you always encouraged him during lectures.

It was a beautiful day with a sea full of emotions and sentiments for us, which left behind a lot of beautiful memories. My wish was fulfilled. Your framed degree is displayed on our front room wall. Whenever I see it I think of my silent, but priceless relationship with Allah (SWT) and I begin to believe in the saying that *"dreams do sometimes come true"*.

I leave you in Allah's (SWT) protection.

Your Mother
Urfana Ayub

Letter No 13.

The purpose of life

Dear Adam,
Peace be upon you.

You know Adam, I have changed a lot or maybe I am changing. This feeling is weighing me down that there is a lot of restlessness, dissatisfaction and a rat race going on around the world. All of this is only to achieve in this life. This is not a preparation for the Hereafter. In fact none of it is for the hereafter. I am getting more and more tired. I have decided to get involved in only those deeds that will help me improve my eternal life. I have lost interest in money and fame. In fact, I am worried that fame and money are attractions of this world. It is difficult to escape their magnetic powers. A staunch faith is mandatory to achieve this.

I often question myself:

Why did Allah (SWT) create me?
What is the purpose of my life?
Am I fulfilling my duties?
Am I fulfilling my duties toward Allah (SWT)?
Am I giving people their rights?
What do I need to do in life and why?
What impact will my actions have on my eternal life?

As time passes I am getting more aware of the fact that we need very little to live our lives, but we try to collect a lot more than we require. What are our basic needs? Food, clothes and shelter! We forget this and set out to build, not one, but many houses or even mansions for ourselves. The irony is that we do not find time to go and sit in each of the rooms in our mansions.

We need food to satiate our hunger and clothes to cover our bodies. But we keep collecting and piling them to an extent that we run out of space. We are humans. Our appetite for worldly things is insatiable.
As a poet said:

There are thousands of desires of heart each more intense
than the other
I fulfilled many of them but it was not enough

Adam, I gave away all of your clothes and shoes to friends and family. Some of them are in Ahmad's use even to this day. You were very fond of trendy and fashionable clothes. But alas, we ignore the truth that each one of us will go away from this world wearing only a white Kafan just like you did.

Why do we spend the prime of our lives and health trying to earn money? We lose our health in this process and suffer from many diseases, and then in our old age we spend this money to regain our health! Adam, if someone has some common sense, they would wonder why do we spend all our time and health in earning money? Isn't there a better use for both these things? We lose our youth as well as health. In old age we finally use up all the money which we had collected in our younger days. So in the end we are left empty-handed.

It took time for me to understand this fact of life, but praise be to Allah it dawned on me finally.

I remember when our house was being renovated, we had just one desire: that our house may be completed according to our desires and wishes. We worked hard for it, spent precious time and money on it, but the thought never crossed our minds that you would not be able to live in this house with us for long. Your room became empty.

Similarly I remember an acquaintance of mine. She had a beautiful mansion fit for royalty that was built for herself Ma Sha Allah. She told me that her husband played a very active role in the completion of every stage of building their house. But after it was finished, he suffered a sudden heart attack and passed away. He did not get a chance to live in the new house with his family that he put so much effort into making. What do we learn from all this? Where are we running and why?

Previously Adam, I was also probably involved in this non-stop race. But your departure from this world jolted me, and instead of running in the race I began to walk. Now sometimes it seems as if I am looking at the world from behind a glass wall where only a few people are present. The glass is absolutely clean and clear. On the other side of the glass, I can see people running around and I can also hear all their noise.

A few days back I attended someone's funeral. The coffin was already present in the hall when I entered. The deceased woman's daughters and other relatives were all standing around the coffin weeping. Lots of people were gathered there, close and distant relatives, neighbours and so on. I took a place in a corner near the wall and began observing the whole scene from behind my glass wall. Except for a few close relatives, the rest of the people were engrossed in worldly gossip. They were inquiring after each other. On one side, the Holy Quran, *Surah Yasin*, Tasbeeh (rosary) and other items of prayer were placed on a shelf, but the women were so absorbed in talking that I felt they had forgotten what sort of occasion they were at. There was a dead body lying there waiting to be buried.

I felt pity at the helplessness of the deceased woman. I prayed for her and began reciting *Surah Yasin*. I looked around and felt like crying out to the people, *"Stop this worldly talk for Allah's (swt) sake. This deceased lady is on her last journey from this world. She needs our prayers. Talk about other things later."*

Adam, we have become very insensitive. The deceased expects prayers from us. He or she is waiting for our prayer before embarking on that final journey. Adam, I feel slightly apprehensive of walking a new path. In these worldly journeys we do find some companions on the way, but if nothing else, we enjoy the journey with the company of a radio or a CD not to feel all alone. But when we depart from this world on the last journey, we have to travel on our own. It must be scary for everyone! May Allah (swt) make our next journey easy for us, Ameen.

Adam, you are very brave to have started on your final journey before your parents or grandparents. I pray to Allah (swt) that may He let us meet you in the Hereafter Ameen.

As a poet said:

After bidding farewell we will keep waiting for them
That one moment will remain in our sight forever
There won't be an evening when your memory did not
knock at the door
There won't be a morning when your face does not glow
for us

Allah Hafiz.

Your Loving Mother,
Urfana Ayub

Letter No 14.

Criticism – A bad attitude

My dear son Adam Ayub,
Peace be upon you.
Lots of love and prayers.

There are many things that I want to share with you. After you went away, Allah (SWT) blessed Mamoon Mohammad with a son, Abdullah, and Uncle Abid with a son, Mohammad. Both children are very cute and everyone is very happy for them.

Now I have become aware that children are one of the most precious blessings of Allah. Healthy children are a priceless treasure of Allah's benevolence, but man is thankless. Instead of thanking Allah (SWT) for His blessings, he is critical of them, like *"Why didn't I get a son instead of a daughter?"* or *"Why isn't the child's complexion fair?"* or *"The baby is not cute enough, isn't healthy, is over or under weight"* etc.

Criticism and grumbling dominate our lives. Our behaviours tend to be more critical than thankful to our Creator. We complain at petty things and about every relation of ours. Not only people, we even grumble with Allah (SWT) that He did not bless us with this or that. We do not try to see what He has given to us praise be to Allah (SWT).

Adam, we have fallen into the habit of protest and complaint. We do not seem to relax until we have whined about something. Our day does not pass without accusation and fault finding.

If we do not find anything worth complaining about, we start blaming the weather. It is cold today, or it is very hot, or why isn't it raining? Or it is heavy wind today and so on. We are never content.

But Adam, these very traits are present in me also. Most of us are like this, but we do not realise it. Now that I have begun to understand it, I am scared. Because Allah (SWT) says, *"the more thankful man is, the more I will give to him"*. If we want Allah (SWT) to grant us more bounties, we must thank Him for what He has already blessed us with.

Allah (SWT) says in the Quran:

"So remember me, I will remember you. And be thankful to me and do not be ungrateful".

Surah Al-Baqarah (The Cow), 2:152

I think one of the reasons why we do not thank Allah (SWT) enough is that we attribute our success to our hard work and forget to give Allah (SWT) due credit. This must be kept in mind at all times; that whatever we have achieved in life is no doubt by Allah's grace first, and then our endeavours. If Allah (SWT) does not give us the ability to do something, we will not be able to do anything. It is imperative that we remember and thank Allah (SWT) at all times.

Sometimes I get very worried and concerned about a certain class of people. They are those who get position and status in this world and who tend to ignore and forget others due to their pride. I get scared of their worldly positions, luxury and lifestyle. In reality this success, money, excessive spending, exalted position in society, costly possessions and respect from others should instil a sense of humility in man. But mostly it is not so. People who are close to Allah (SWT) thank Him, while other people become proud and boastful. They do not treat the poor as human and they forget that every soul has to return to Allah (SWT) where we will be answerable for each of our actions and deeds.

As Allah (SWT) says in the Holy Quran:

"Beautified is the life of this world for those who disbelieve, and they ridicule those who believe. But those who fear Allah are above them on the day of Resurrection. And Allah awards whom He wills without measure".

Surah Al-Baqarah (The Cow), 2:212

Adam, no matter what a person gets, he/she is never thankful. He/she wants more. Today I met a person who had only one arm. From a distance it appeared that he had concealed his arm in his jacket, but when he came close, I was distressed to see that there was no arm beyond his shoulder. He was busy working with his other arm.

Praise be to Allah, how can I thank Allah (SWT). I think of myself, who used to complain even if the water becomes cold during Wudhu (ablution). Yet this man with only one arm is working in our society alongside everyone else, without considering himself as disabled and without looking for others' sympathies Masha'Allah.

O Allah (SWT), make us rely on you and you alone. Make us turn only to You, may we always ask help from You alone.

Let whining and complaining disappear from our lives completely and make us thank You with our every breath, Ameen.

Adam I leave you in Allah's (SWT) protection.

Your Mother,
Urfana Ayub

Letter No 15.

Memories and Butterflies

Dear son Adam.
Lots of love and prayers.

Five years have passed since you went away. My relationship with you has kept on strengthening each year. In the life of this world you are now 23 years old. I want to share a poem with you which I wrote three years after your departure.

The first year without you, I know how I spent
This was a difficult time and my heart grieved, I can never forget
Tears were falling ceaselessly
My heart would jump at every footstep
Patience came after lots of supplication
Anxieties knocked on my heart abound
I told my heart at every sound that
The truth was that you were gone
The second year which passed, yes I know
Time was trying and my heart grieved, how can I forget
Tears had found abode in my eyes
My heart was scared of every sound
My soul's grief was lessening
Allah's (SWT) wisdom was dawning on me
I had compromised with the truth
That you had gone for forever
The third year which passed, I know how
My relation with you has changed
This truth revealed a lot to me
This truth taught me a lot

Tears now no longer know me
They seem strangers if even if they come near me

(Urfana Ayub, 25th December 2012)

Adam, memories are strange things. Some moments and faces are engraved on our minds. They seem like dreams. They come, stay for some time with us and then flee. They keep flying like butterflies. I remember in my childhood I loved to catch butterflies. I used to run after them in my mother's lawn, but it was not easy to catch them, because when I approached them, they would fly away and sit on another flower. Memories are somewhat similar. You can't catch them even if you want to.

Your memory and your perception are like a fragrance which I cannot confine, but I feel it all around me. It is difficult to understand this emotion.

Adam, as a Muslim, I know that these letters will never reach you; neither can you hear what I say. But it is a very gratifying feeling that you are close to me and I can still say all those things to you that I would have had you been alive.
As a poet said:

Those faces which dwell in my heart like fragrance
Cannot be separated from my mind or sight
Why can't I find escape from my memories?
Why doesn't he part from me even after his departure?

I have finally understood this feeling, Adam. The people who are close to you and live in your heart will always be near you, whether they actually live near or far away. Yet there are also people who are far from you even though they live in your house or town. This is so because your hearts are far apart from each other. Likewise, people close to your heart will always be near you even if they are on the other side of the globe.

Adam, do you remember a friend of mine who lives in America? So many years have passed since our marriages, but our friendship is still like it was in college days in Pakistan. Even if we talk to each other once or twice a year, it never occurs to us that we live so far apart or are getting connected after so long.

A few years back I met Aunty Tasneem in Pakistan after a gap of fifteen years. It did not strike us for one moment that we were meeting after so many years. Likewise, many people and relatives live in our hearts, you are also one of those people who has grown close to me even after departing. And now you are so close that you dwell in my heart.

Everyone talks about you in the house. You know that Allah (SWT) blessed Mamoon Kaleem with a son after you. They named him Adam so that your name continues to be part of our family. Young Adam is a cute boy, Masha 'Allah. May Allah (SWT) grant him health and integrity of faith, Ameen.

May you be in Allah's (SWT) protection my son.

Your Mother, Urfana Ayub

Letter No 16.

Time

Dear son Adam Ayub,
Peace be upon you.
Lots of love and prayers.

Yesterday, I met someone whose sister-in-law fell from the roof and passed away. She was pregnant and close to her delivery time. The whole incident happened suddenly and killed both the mother and her unborn child. This tragedy caused such a mental shock to the deceased woman's mother that she went into a coma.

Adam, I often think that when we hear of such occurrences we realise that man is completely powerless. One moment can change our lives. No doubt such accidents are a big test from Allah (SWT) for the deceased's family and relatives.

There is a lesson in it for us who are around, but we do not pay much heed to it. We may mourn for the deceased's family for some time, but tend to forget the incident very quickly indeed. We do not learn the real lesson which these accidents teach. Or we have become so insensitive that we think *"It is their test, not ours"*. Why don't we realise, that if someone is passing through a test today, Allah (SWT) may put me through a similar test tomorrow? How can I absorb the lesson which should be learnt from it?

The most common excuse for this is *"We do not have time"*. Working women and housewives are both so busy in their

85

work that they say they do not get time. Adam, I would like to know then, who does have time? Sometime I think there is no space left in our time.

But what about those people who are serving their religion? Do they have 40 or 50 hours in one day? No! The truth is that everyone is allocated exactly 24 hours in a day. Neither one hour more nor one less. If everyone is given the same amount of time, then where lies the difference? I thought a lot about this and came to the conclusion that the difference is in the importance we give to time. The more important a particular activity is for somebody, the more time and priority he will give to it. In the past people did not have watches, but everyone had time. Today, everyone possesses a watch, but nobody has time.

We do not have time for our religion, for connection with Allah (SWT), for Salah, for recitation and understanding of Quran, but we have time for all our worldly activities like cooking, clothes, spouses, children, job, home, car, education and success and connecting with other people. We are so engrossed in these that we do not find time for any other thing.
As a poet said:

This worldly wealth, this relation and belonging
These idols of illusion and suspicion, La Illaha IllAllah

(Allama Iqbal)

Adam, I try to figure out those activities of my life that cause me to be negligent towards Allah (SWT). What are those tasks which rob me of my precious time and ability? It is Allah's (SWT) promise that He will test us by granting us His bounties and blessings. Now it is our duty to be vigilant as to how we live our lives. We must not let ourselves be so absorbed in worldly relationships and material things that we forget our duty towards our Creator. I have made up my mind that for Allah's sake, Insha'Allah, I will forgo all those habits and hobbies which are for worldly benefits and all those activities which consume my precious time, money and ability, but do not provide any benefit in the Hereafter.

Adam, you know I have many pastimes. These hobbies demand a lot of time. But now, as my understanding of religion is increasing, I am giving more value to time. I have realised that the most precious of all worldly things is TIME. It is more valuable than our money and other assets, but alas we do not give importance to it!

Allah (SWT) says in *Surah Al-Asr*:

"Promise by time. Verily Man is in loss, except those who have Faith, and do righteous deeds, and persuade one another to truth and persuade one another to Patience."

Surah Al-Asr (The Time), 103:1-3

May Allah (SWT) guide us to value time and may He give scope and dimension to our time, Ameen.

I leave you in Allah's (SWT) protection my son.

Your Mother,
Urfana Ayub

Letter No 17.

Ilm (Knowledge)

My dear son Adam Ayub,
Peace be upon you.
Infinite love and prayers for you.

I wanted to tell you that your brothers and sister have grown up considerably since you went away. Masha'Allah, Arslan has passed his driving test. Yesterday, he drove the car independently for the first time. I was elated at his achievement. First he dropped Ahmad to the Madrassa (Mosque) and then went to meet Dadi Jan and Baba. Masha'Allah he is doing all that you had planned to do before him. May Allah (SWT) grant him a life of conviction (Imaan), Ameen.

A parents relationship with their children is very beautiful. It is entirely selfless. Parents love their children with all their hearts and being. They pray for their children's success at each step and stage of life. It is my belief that, though fortune, work and endeavours play a vital role in one's life second only to Allah's (SWT) blessings, parents' intense and sincere prayers are a great asset in our lives. After Allah's (SWT) will, our success is dependent on our parents' prayers.

Adam, I also feel that children do not give parents their rightful love and credit until they become parents themselves and sometimes not even then. Children tend to be selfish, whereas parents can never be. Children's love for their parents may decrease, but a parents' love is like a priceless diamond.

I
remember when you were admitted to nursery. I was very happy as if you had done something extraordinary, or that in the whole wide world only my Adam was the one who had gone to nursery. Then the next step was your entry into a fulltime school. My pride and happiness kept increasing at each step. As you kept getting older and completed different landmarks of your education and life itself, I used to rejoice silently in the fact that my child was growing up.

I very well remember that when you got admitted to college my happiness was boundless. When anybody asked about you, I used to reply with joy and pride that *"My son goes to college".* Then came the next step - you went to university. Again, my elation could not be described merely in the words: *"My son was studying for a degree programme".* When I think of it, Adam, you were not doing anything extraordinary in this world. In reality, you were actually doing the same as most children of your age.

But, being your mother, all my happiness was linked with you and your success. I believe that it is not only me - all mothers feel the same. Now I feel this way about Arslan.

But your sudden departure makes me consider the fact that these successes, promotions and achievements are for this world only. This world and our life is a path which leads towards our destination, but we must remember that this world is not our destination. This path is so colourful, so beautiful and lively that we lose ourselves in it. We forget that it is only a path, not our destination.

Adam, Allah (SWT) gives a new colour to our lives when He wills, just like He gave to my life by summoning you back to Him. I had never thought you would go like this, or so soon. No parents ever wants or can even think that their children will die before them.

Adam, now what makes me happy is that your brothers and sister will get a worldy education, along with a full understanding of religion. If any one of them is called back to our Creator at any time, at least I will be satisfied that I had not only educated them for this world, but I had also trained them in matters pertaining to our religion and for their hereafter.

I pray to Allah (SWT) to forgive me for any shortcomings in your upbringing and education on my part. May He exalt your position in Heaven, Ameen.

I want Arslan, Ahmad and Ambar to succeed in life and to be well-educated, but more than this I want them to be preachers of our religion, in that they should learn and teach Islam. I also want them to follow Islam in practical life, to have the best of manners and be role models for their friends and companions.

All human beings are dead. Only those are alive who have knowledge
All the learned people are asleep. Only those are awake who practice it
All those who practice are losers. Only those are benefiting who are sincere in it
All sincere people are in danger. Only those are successful

90

who are devoid of arrogance

(Al Ghazali)

We all try to gain knowledge, but only a few use it. Only those people can practise it who sincerely work for it. No matter how many books you load onto a donkey, the volumes will not change him in any practical way. Similarly, no matter how many books we read, courses we complete or degrees we achieve, they are nothing but pieces of paper unless they mould our deeds in a positive direction and until the knowledge assimilates in our being.

As someone very effectively said:

"To attain knowledge only and not practice it is just like doing Wudhoo (ablution) all your life and not offering Salah. What good is ablution if it is not followed by Salah? It is said that a sensible man is not the one who talks big, but the one who can understand small things".

We need to think about this universe. We need to understand these small things. Adam, I am surprised at my own self. Previously, when I used to look at the sky, it did not evoke any special feeling in me. But now when I look at it, its beauty and magnificence, the movement of clouds and the charming colours of the Heavens take me to another world and I am forced to think about this. I am thankful to Allah (SWT) for having given me this perception. But Adam, this came about because of you. Ever since you went into the grave, I have been forced to think and meditate. There was no other option left for me.

As Allah (SWT) says in the Holy Quran:

"Haven't they looked into the governance of heavens and earth and all that Allah has created? And it may well be that their term is close by. Then in what message, after this, will they believe?"

Surah Al-A'raf (The Heights), 7:185

May you be in Allah's (SWT) protection my son.

Your Mother, Urfana Ayub

Violation of Allah's (SWT) system

My dear son, Adam,
Lots of love and prayer.

There is something stuck in my mind since yesterday. Adam, it takes many years for someone to build their reputation in society. But sometimes this respect can be lost in a moment due to one's negligence and stupidity. I pray to Allah (SWT) that may He safeguard our dignity and respect, Ameen.

When someone realises his mistake and returns to Allah (SWT), repents and asks for Allah's (SWT) forgiveness, it is hoped that he will be pardoned if Allah (SWT) so wills. But his fellow human beings do not forgive him. It is easy to please Allah (SWT), but very difficult to please people.

We, on the other hand, spend our whole lives trying to please people and keep them happy. Adam, sometimes I think that if we showed the same amount of love, respect, regard and obedience to Allah (SWT) as we did to some people, we might be able to gain access to Heaven. But we do not understand. We keep chasing people. We are totally on the wrong track. We are ignorant of the only being who we must please. Instead we give importance to those fake people who do not give a penny's credit to us. At times I think that we are going against Allah's (SWT) system.

Our Creator says to us:

• Believe in one Allah (SWT) - we know that Allah (SWT) is one and only, but we do not follow His commands.

• Be fair even if it causes loss to you yet we are more concerned about our gain; we do not care about fair play.

• Be just – we do not know what on earth justice is.

• Do not lie – untruthfulness is in our blood and we utter lies without hesitation.

• Do not show off – we want to show off our every good deed.

• Be tolerant – we complain all the time and do not even think of our blessings.

• Do not show anger – we get angry at petty things, totally ignoring patience and gratitude.

• Be thankful – we always ask for more than we get without any feeling of gratitude.

• Be humble – we walk on this earth with pride and arrogance.

• Fear Allah (SWT) - we fear people for no reason.

• Rest at night – we keep awake at night for no reason. Work and earn during the day – we sleep all morning and get up late.

- Perform Hajj – we go abroad every year for holidays, but do not perform Umrah or Hajj.

- Meditate on Allah's (SWT) power and might – we are bewitched by modern technology.

- Look at the skies and ponder on them – we are impressed by tall buildings.

- Eat pure and clean food – we eat unhealthy fast food, smoke and drink alcohol.

As Allama Iqbal said:

How you abhor getting up early in the morning
You do not love Me, you just can't part with your sleep
Your free nature is burdened by the limitations of Ramadhan
Say is this your pact of allegiance?
Nation is formed on religion –if there is no religion there is
no identity for you
If there is no mutual attraction (gravity) then this galaxy of
stars cannot exist

There are some people who do not even fulfil their religious obligations willingly. Mixed emotions are seen, especially when it comes to payment of Zakat. Some people find it hard to part with a portion of that money which Allah (SWT) has given to them and give it to the needy. Although it is clearly stated in the Quran, donate money to the poor from that which has been given to you by Allah (SWT).

When Hadhrat Abu Bakr Siddique (RA) became the Caliph of Muslims, he decided to do Jihad against those people who refused to pay Zakat. Some of the Sahaba (companions of Prophet Muhammad (PBUH)) objected to this, saying, *"Will you do Jihad against those people who pray five times a day and observe fast in the month of Ramadhan?"* Abu Bakr (RA) replied, *"Those who do not pay their dues in Zakat are doubtlessly cast out of the circle of Islam because, without the payment of Zakat, even the Salah remains suspended (is not accepted by Allah)."*

Hadrat Abu Bakr's (RA) decision to do Jihad against the non-payers of Zakat is enough to highlight its importance in a Muslim's life.

When it comes to Hajj, people try to evade the issue, saying *"We will go when Allah (SWT) summons us"* and do not make any effort. They believe that, unless a miracle happens, they will not proceed to Hajj. I am amazed at these people Adam, because many of them have visited different countries for their holidays. They save for and plan their vacations. But when it comes to religious obligations, the general notion is *"We will do it when Allah wills"* or *"When he calls us"*.

Adam, why do they forget that Allah will do it only when they themselves want it and strive for it? Allah (SWT) knows the secrets of our hearts. We cannot hide anything from Him, but still our actions are different from what we have inside our heart. We know that Allah is very well aware of our intentions, but still we claim not to be hypocrites?

As a poet said:

> *Not a few show me just one person*
> *Who is alike from inside and out*

Adam, I request to Allah (SWT) that may He make us all, including me, the same on the outside and inside, and may He grant us sincerity in all that we do, Ameen.

May you be in Allah's (SWT) protection my son.

Your Mother, Urfana Ayub

The Great Mothers

Dear Adam,
Lots of love and prayers for you my child.

Adam we talked a lot about you today. I met two of my friends whose mothers have come from Pakistan. Both these friends had read *Taray Janay Kay Baad* and they shared their views about the book with me. Alahamdulilah you have connected me with so many people.

I could never have become such a strong link to anybody's personal life story had you not gone away from this world. On the one hand, I sometimes feel that you are still here with me, and on the other it seems that yes, you have indeed left us. Because while leaving, you connected me to this world and its reality, to people and their sorrows. This connection is that sort of link where people usually remark, *"I have met you for the first time, but it seems as if I already know you and have met you before".*

Do you know, Adam, how those people know me? They know Adam's mother; they know the author of *Taray Janay Kay Baad*. People give me lots of love and respect. That is why I say that you have not left us even after death. All parents want to earn respect because of their children. Masha'Allah Adam you fulfilled this obligation when you were alive, and even after death you are fulfilling this duty beautifully and completely, Praise be to Allah (SWT).

Adam, some people pass through difficulties many times in life. Allah (SWT) tests them repeatedly. I pray that may Allah (SWT) keep these people steadfast and strong in trying times, Ameen.

Today I met two such strong and splendid personalities. The first woman lost her husband suddenly, a few years after her marriage. Then, when her only son reached seventeen years of age, he died in an accident. She experienced many sorrows apart from these in life as well.

The second person is a woman whose husband died young and she spent the rest of her life as a widow taking care of her three children. After meeting these people, I felt that the woman who lived with her husband for only a few years sacrificed the rest of her life for the happiness of her three children. She takes care of each and every need for her children. I pay homage and tribute to such mothers.

Our mothers are not selfish. They have every right to remarry, but what prevents them from doing so? It is their maternal instinct and their selfless love for their children. Otherwise they too would like to share their life with someone, to share their happiness and their sorrows, to have a partner who would dispel their loneliness and be a sincere friend, but they sacrifice everything for the sake of their children.

Yet children can be very selfish and greedy. They use their parents for their own benefit. They only maintain relationships until the parents are useful to them, but as soon as the benefits cease, the relationship also dies. I heard of a woman whose widowed mother-in-law brought up her son on her own. She very lovingly took care of him

99

and his needs, but the daughter-in-law prevented the son from meeting his mother. The daughter-in-law was so possessive that when her husband died, she did not even allow the mother to have a last look at her son's face before burial. I fail to understand how people can be so heartless. Allah *(SWT)* says in the holy Quran:

"And your Lord has decreed that you not worship/obey except Him, and to parents, good treatment. And if one or both of them reach old age during your lifetime say not to them [so much as], "uff," and do not chide them but speak to them words of respect. And lower to them the wing of humility out of mercy with a tender heart and say, "My Lord, have mercy upon them as they brought me up [when I was] small." Your Lord is most knowing of what is within yourselves. If you should be righteous - then indeed He is ever, to the often returning [to Him], Forgiving".

Surah Al-Isra' (The Journey by Night)/Bani Israel (Children of Israel) 17:23-25

Adam, I fail to comprehend why such beautiful relationships cause so much pain and grief that even the souls get injured. As someone wisely said, *"Relationships are like seasons, extremely good at times, and intolerable at others"*. The difference between the two is that seasons affect our body and relationships hurt our souls.

Adam, it is my prayer that may Allah (SWT) give us the ability to keep our relationships alive, the wisdom to maintain difficult relationships and the insight to keep our close links, Ameen.

Adam, I have full faith that relationships are important, not money or things. Sometimes we give so much importance to material things that relationships break. We do not realise when cracks appear in our relationships. Every relationship is as delicate as porcelain. The more fragile it is, the more care it demands. We can buy and achieve all the worldly things, but the sanctity of relationships can never be regained at any cost.

Our beloved Prophet Muhammad (PBUH) said:

"Maintaining relations is not doing good in response to good gestures, but a true guardian of relations is a person who tries to maintain a relationship even when the other party is bent upon breaking them"

(Narrated in Bukhari)

Your Mother,
Urfana Ayub

Letter No 20.

We will have to go when we have to go

Dear son Adam Ayub,
Lots of love and prayers to you my child.

Adam, today your youngest brother Ahmad has turned sixteen years of age, Masha'Allah.

When you left us he was just an eleven-year-old boy. Now Masha'Allah, he is a tall, young man. On occasions like these I want to share my feelings with you.

These are all Allah's (SWT) blessings, praise be to Allah I do not deserve them, but it is Allah's (SWT) benevolence and magnanimity that He has given me all the blessings of the world. I cannot count Allah's (SWT) bounties. Ahmad is a very sweet and loving boy. Had you been here, you too would have liked to spend time with him. It is my humble prayer to Allah (SWT) to grant him a life filled with health and Imaan, Ameen.

I was talking to someone this morning whose husband often complained about pain in his stomach and back. A few days back he was diagnosed with stomach cancer, which was at its last stage. She was very depressed. Only a few days earlier one of her cousins had a roadside accident. He was a healthy man with no illness whatsoever. He was planning to go to Pakistan from Saudi Arabia on holidays, but unfortunately, he had an accident before his flight and died instantly.

Adam, death is inevitable. Illness and accidents are all various causes of death, but the bare truth is that wherever a person is destined to die, death will happen at that particular spot. We cannot question it, but I feel that most people are terrified of diseases like cancer and they think that they will die because of it. But it is not like this, Adam! It is possible for a cancer patient to live for six months, one year or even more. But a healthy person with no diseases can die in an instant. We humans do not have the power or knowledge to predict the time when our own body, which we always think of as our possession, will be separated from its soul and embark on the journey of death!

Alahamdolilah, no illnesses worry me now because I believe that we will have to go when we have to go. I wonder why people do not understand this! Our lives would be so much easier if we only realised, Insha'Allah.

Adam, the gist of the matter is our relationship with Allah (SWT). When we are tense and restless, we try to look for that "rope" which we take for "Allah's rope". If our relationship with Allah (SWT) is strong then praise be to Allah none of the diseases, tests or difficulties will break us, but if this relationship is weak then Satan overpowers us and takes us in the other direction.

Adam, Nani Ammi says that we should pray to Allah (SWT) to keep us steadfast on Imaan till our deaths, Ameen. We are passing through a difficult time when a Muslim finds it hard to remain resolute on his religion and faith.

I was talking to an acquaintance who told me that her husband was a pious and religious man, but for some time he has become ignorant of his religion.

May Allah (SWT) protect us all from these difficult situations. An abundance of faith is the best possession a Muslim can hope for. There is nothing more precious than this. Similarly, our love for Allah (SWT) should be the strongest love and bond in all our relationships. When loving people, there is always an element of apprehension that the person may change or betray us and one lives an entire life under this fear. On the contrary, our relationship with Allah (SWT) is free of this fear.

As a poet said:

How easy is loving you, O Lord
There is no question of betrayal, no fear of separation

Adam, man's relationship with his Creator is the sincerest of all, but we do not make any sacrifice for it. Just like our worldly ties sometimes demand a sacrifice to determine who is faithful and who is not, Allah (SWT) also tests us in this world to determine who has more faith and trust in Him. We will not get heaven for nothing. This heaven is very expensive; we will have to strive for it and earn it. I pray to Allah (SWT) to grant true guidance to us, Ameen.

Allah Hafiz my dear son Adam Ayub.

Your Mother, Urfana Ayub

Letter No 21.

What type of soil are we made of?

Dear son Adam Ayub,
Lots of love and prayers for you my son.

Your mother misses you a lot son! A few days back I attended a charity function where the American black Muslim Malcolm X's youngest daughter was the chief guest. Malcolm X died before her birth, but even fifty years after her father's death, all his children are engaged in the completion of his mission.

Malcolm X's life is a bright example for many people. I often contemplate whether it is possible for a single person to bring about a revolution by his efforts and actions. I am surprised that yes, he can, but where are the rest of them? Our beloved Prophet Muhammad (PBUH) brought true guidance for all mankind which can enlighten our hearts too. Allah (SWT) has made man *Ashraf-ul-Makhlooqat*; that is, His most superior creation. He has given us a brain, the ability to see and hear; He gave us arms, legs and a body. But unfortunately, only a few people utilise the intelligence and comprehension which Allah (SWT) has bestowed upon us. Even today people around the world acknowledge the efforts and endeavours of Malcolm X, and that he was the first American black Muslim to perform Hajj, Ma Sha Allah. May Allah (SWT) exalt his status and give him a place in Jannat-ul-Firdous, Ameen.

Adam I am really impressed by those people who are prepared to forgo everything for their religion, like their previous religion, their blood relatives and their homes. These people are very courageous and great. It is said that when a person makes up his mind to follow his religion resolutely, Allah (SWT) tests his faith to see whether he is sincere in his efforts or not. It does not take thousands of people to bring about a revolution; even a single man's faith and sincere efforts can bear fruit. Our beloved Prophet Muhammad (PBUH), the four great Caliphs and the Prophet's companions were all such people who never lost sight of their goal, no matter what circumstances and difficulties came their way. The whole history of Islam is filled with such glorious examples, but very sorrowfully it has to be admitted that such examples are rarely seen anymore. This is because no one thinks of religion as their obligation. Everyone tries to ascribe this duty to others.

Adam, I was also like this previously, but now I have begun to comprehend things a little better and so my thoughts have changed.

When we think of donating money or other assets to charity, we do not consider it to be the obligation of only the more affluent and successful people in our society. This duty is equally mine. Whether I have less money or heaps of it, whatever I give in charity will benefit me, just as charity given by other people will benefit them.

I have seen that when parents get old and weak, many children turn away from them and put the parental responsibility onto other siblings because they are better off or closer to the parents. Adam, the reality is that parents belong to all the children, so it is the responsibility of all the children to look after them and care for them. Only the children who take care of their parents and keep them happy, whether they live close to their parents or abroad, whether they are rich or poor, will be successful if they strive wholeheartedly to do their best and with full sincerity.

If we want real success, then we must be in business with Allah (SWT). Everyone is worried about this world's business. How to start it, what steps should be taken to enhance it and so on, but now, Adam, I want to do business with Allah (SWT). The difference is that when we do trade with our Creator, we do not get the profit at once. All of it keeps collecting in our account with Allah (SWT). But the biggest benefit of trading with Allah (SWT) is that He will never betray us, Nauzobillah (Allah forbid). It is guaranteed that there will not be any losses, and the profit is promised to be not one hundred percent, but up to seven hundred times. Is there any other trader or any businessman who would give so much profit and conduct business with so much honesty?

In the trade of this world people try to deceive each other. Even real brothers are no exception, and children can betray their parents! May Allah (SWT) give us the integrity to be honest, so that we can change our measure of fairness, Ameen.

A non-Muslim, when offering job to a Muslim, asked him *"Do you regularly offer Salah?"* The Muslim asked the reason for this question. The non-Muslim replied, *"I want to see whether you are faithful towards your Creator, because if you are sincere with Him you will be sincere with me also"*. Adam, very few people, including myself, are faithful. If we are not faithful with Allah (SWT) who blesses us with each and every bounty, who grants life and breathe to us, then how can we be honest with people?

As a poet said:

> *Test your soil before sowing the seed*
> *As sincerity is not in the nature of every land*

We all must try to find out what type of soil we are made of!

May you be in Allah's (SWT) protection my child.

Your Mother,
Urfana Ayub

Letter No 22.

Search

My dear son Adam Ayub,
Peace be upon you.

Someone sent me this Dua (prayer) which I liked very much.

Search

I search for your approval at each step of my life
O Allah (SWT) I seek for excellence in my love for you
I am embedded in sins, fallen on earth
I search for the prayer which will cleanse me of my sins
Whatever I did was wrong, I am the cause for my own
destruction
I search for the action O Lord by which I will gain your
appreciation.
(Ameen)

Adam, I often ask myself, what is man in seeking? Is desire another name for seeking? Maybe not, I don't know...

Generally speaking, man is in search of a sound future, a good life partner, success, children and the comforts of this life. Man, desires these things and sometimes this desire turns into a struggle. When I think about myself, I feel man's search keeps changing with time and his insights into life. Success also lies in changing oneself, as we all achieve greater understanding over the years.

Since childhood I have sought good friends and companions, because I feel that a person is known by the company he/she keeps. This search of mine still continues. But another search, which is more intense and an ever-growing process, is the search for peace of mind. It is one of the great blessings of Allah (SWT).

I seek the will and pleasure of my Creator, so that He will be pleased with me, and I accept His every decision wholeheartedly. I seek that prayer which will be accepted by my Lord and that He may distance me from evil. I seek all those good deeds, doing which I may be able to please Allah (SWT).

I very much like the Dua, which our beloved Prophet (PBUH) used to recite *Dua e Istaftah* (the opening Dua) after *Takbeer-e-Tehreema* in Salah.

"Oh Lord put that much distance between me and my sins as is present between East and West. Oh Allah! (SWT) cleanse me of my sins like a white cloth is cleansed of its dust and dirt. Oh Lord wash away my sins with water, ice and hailstones."

Adam, I feel that most of our lives are spent trying to achieve worldly pleasures. That point comes in only a few people's lives when one sets out on a journey to search for his own self, his Creator and peace of mind. I think Allah's special blessings and mercy are with that person whom Allah (SWT) engages to search for Him.

I have come to the conclusion that discovering Allah (SWT) is not that difficult. He resides in our own hearts. One only needs to look at one's heart and find Him. The more we want to achieve something, the more effort we will make to get it. The whole universe is filled with signs of Allah (SWT).

As Allah (SWT) says in *Surah Ar-Rahman*:

"He made flow the two seas, meeting [side by side]; between them is a barrier, neither of them transgresses."

Surah Ar-Rahman (The Most Gracious), 55:19-20.

Adam, I feel that for me these verses of the Qur'an are enough to discover and recognise Allah (SWT). My Lord kept the waters of two seas separate from one another by maintaining a partition between them. Otherwise how is it possible that two bodies of water can be side-by-side without mixing? Praise be to Allah, for me this is the search for Allah (SWT) and the discovery of Him in a real sense. We cannot succeed in life or the hereafter without discovering Allah (SWT).

I am also very much impressed by our fingerprints. There are billions of people on earth, but no two people have identical fingerprints. It is not a matter of chance! The markings on our fingers are an example of Allah's (SWT) creativity. It is not a masterpiece created by an Artist.

"Does the man think that We will not assemble his bones? Why not! [We are] Able to restore his very fingertips."

Surah Al-Qiyamah (The Resurrection), 75:3-4.

Adam, doesn't this point compel us to accept the oneness of Allah (SWT)? The signs of Allah's (SWT) greatness and might are scattered all around us. We only need to possess that sight which will see them.

My errors know no boundaries
Your grace has no limits
Neither can one count my mistakes
Nor your blessings

It is my heartiest prayer, Adam, that may we all be able to find our creator. All those who are ignorant; may Allah (SWT) guide them towards the path of His discovery (Ameen).

May Allah (SWT) be your guardian my son.

Your Mother,
Urfana Ayub

Identifying good and bad friends

My very dear son Adam Ayub.
Peace be upon you.
Lots of love and prayers.

Adam, sometimes we develop a very strong relationship with certain people; a relationship which has no name. It is not necessary that these people are our blood relatives. Blood relations are made by Allah (SWT). We cannot change them. There is no substitute for parents in this world. Similarly one cannot change one's siblings. Matrimonial relationships also must be maintained and kept alive. We cannot break ties with our near and distant relatives either; but out of all these people there are some who are very close to our heart, even though they are miles away.

Some people's fine nature and polished etiquette are impressive. There is so much sincerity and love in their dealings with people that they touch the heart. Praise be to Allah Adam, I am a very lucky and rich person in this regard. Allah (SWT) has always kept me surrounded by such pure people. I've always prayed to Allah (SWT) that He may grant me and my children the company of sincere people. May He let us meet pious people and may He bless us with closeness to the best of people. Let such people be my friends who would enhance my Imaan, and let me be such a person whose company is beneficial for others.

Somebody once rightly remarked that, *"I have only two friends; first Allah (SWT) and second that person who keeps me connected with Allah's (SWT) love and does not let me ignore it"*. I also want to be such a friend, Adam, who makes other people associate with Allah (SWT). Good and pious people are a blessing of Allah (SWT). There are many examples around me where a person became close to Allah (SWT) because of a friend. Allah (SWT) guided him towards the right path. On the other hand, even just one individual, a bad friend, may lead a person away from the right path.

Our Prophet (PBUH) said,

"A good and a bad friend are likened to a perfume vendor and an ironmonger who works with fire. You will gain something from a perfume vendor's company; either you will buy perfume or you will get its fragrance. On the other hand an ironmonger's fire will burn your house or clothes or its bad smell will reach your mind".

(Bukhari, Muslim)

On another occasion our beloved Prophet (PBUH) remarked,

"Every man follows the religion of his friend. Thus everyone must be mindful of whom he is befriending".

(Musnad Ahmad, Mishkah)

We are concerned about our children that they may remain on the right path and make decent friends. But we forget the same for our own selves. We need good friends and sincere, selfless people at every stage of our lives. Friendships with such people are very precious. We cannot buy them with

114

money. We can purchase many worldly belongings, but not sincere friends. We need to be thankful to Allah (SWT) that He blessed us with this gift, Praise be to Allah .

Adam, do you know where and how I found these beautiful and sincere friends, or who caused me to meet these great people that enriched my life? It was Allah's (SWT) best gift to humanity, the source of all knowledge and guidance - the glorious Qur'an. The people whom I met after getting connected to the Qur'an are in reality my honest and sincere friends, because they are not concerned with my worldly status and neither am I bothered about theirs. I pray to Allah (SWT) that may He grant them peace and success in this world. Likewise, they too wish well for me.

Actually, our real concern is the hereafter. I want success for my friends in the hereafter. The Qur'an has completely changed the measure of my friendships. If I am not concerned about the eternal life of my friends and I simply want to benefit from their status in this world, then I consider myself to be selfish.

We are concerned all the time about worldly things like our house, car, degree, job, status and so on, but we have completely forgotten our afterlife. Adam, real friends are only those who make you think about your eternal life, who urge their friends to make preparations and who walk with them as companions to find the path which will lead them to their chosen destination, Heaven.

Our beloved Prophet Muhammad (PBUH) remarked:

"There are a few chosen people of Allah (SWT) who are neither

prophets nor Shaheed, but Allah (SWT) will exalt them to such a place that even Allah's (SWT) messengers and the Shuhada will envy their position".

The Prophet's companions asked, *"Who are these lucky people, O Prophet?"* He (PBUH) answered, *"They are those people who love each other only for the sake of Allah's (SWT) religion. They are neither related by blood nor is there any monetary connection between them. I swear by Allah (SWT) that on the Day of Judgement not only their faces would be radiant with light but their whole being would be made of light. And when the human race will be petrified with fear, these people will neither be afraid nor sad on any account."*

Then the Prophet (PBUH) recited the following verse of the Qur'an:

"Listen carefully! No doubt, there is no fear nor any grief upon the allies of Allah."

Surah Yunus (Prophet Jonah), 10:62.

O Lord, let me and all my friends die in a state of Imaan, and protect us from sudden death. Let us die in a state of purity whilst reciting Kalimah. Let us have the Kafan and the grave. Let me be a source of permanent reward for them and them for me.

Allah Hafiz my son.

Your Mother,
Urfana Ayub

Attitudes of people

My very dear friend and son,
Peace be upon you.
Lots of love and prayers.

Do you know what date it is today Adam? According to the English calendar, it is 27th December - exactly five years since you were buried. Nothing stopped after you. Years, months, weeks, days and moments kept passing. There were times when I felt that I would stop breathing; that I would not be able to live without you. But Adam, my breathing did not stop. When a mother's life keeps on going, then how could the rest of the system stop? Allah (SWT) has His own system and everything in this world works according to and under its control.

Five years ago 27th December coincided with 10th Muharram and the day was a Sunday. This year 10th Muharram was on 3rd November, and today, 27th December falls on a Saturday. Everything has changed. I am missing you very much today. It is the same every year, as if my heart is able to read the date and get sad. Maybe every mother's heart is like this that tears flow uncontrollably!

Our whole family went to stay for a few days with your Mamoon in London. It has been a long time since we did so and it felt nice to see everybody. Mamoon's children are growing up. Praise be to Allah, I was overjoyed when Abdul Wahab gave me a card where he had written your name alongside the rest of the children. I badly felt your absence. Even now when I have to call Arslan and Ahmad, I call out your name before theirs. I sent the following text message to all the family members on your behalf!

"Salaam everyone, Another year has passed after me. Time is flying! It does not wait for anything or anybody. It simply reminds me that five years ago I was also a part of your lives and lived in this world. Then all of a sudden I was called back!

Please think of your own departure and make preparations for it. Never forget the purpose of your creation. Do not get engrossed in this world. Remember to pray for me and my family."

Adam I want your memory to teach us the fact that we are not going to live in this world forever and we have to worry about the hereafter. We should never forget the purpose of our lives.

This time we explored London thoroughly. The beauty of the tall buildings reminded us that there are many attractions in this world. We are lost in the allure of these skyscrapers, giant wheels and gardens.

While admiring a tall, beautiful, glass-covered building, we do not perceive the height of the sky, the changing colours of the atmosphere. We ignore the different types of birds flying. We do not feel the cool breeze flowing. Why? We do not have time to think about Allah's (SWT) creations whose magnificence is free for everyone to enjoy. We are more keen to see the things which man has made from the raw materials provided by Allah (SWT), even if it means buying tickets to see them.

Allah (SWT) says in the Holy Qur'an:

"Holy and Exalted is He! High above all that they say! The seven heavens and the earth, and all beings therein, declare His glory: And there is nothing, which might not speak of His Glory praising Him but you do not understand their [way of] exalting. Verily He is ever Forbearing Most Forgiving!"

Surah Al-Isra' (The Journey by Night)/Bani Israel (Children of Israel) 17:43-44)

Allah (SWT) has created a complete human being whose mind and all other organs work with perfection. Yet we make a special trip to look at statues resembling humans which are carved by human hands. Then we applaud the artists who made these statues, but our mind does not wander to the Supreme Creator who made man in the first place!

There are people in this world who are fully aware of the purpose behind their creation and they are even ready to combat the deception of Satan and fight the evil of their own egos. I envy these people Adam!

There is another category of people who can see the right path, but they do not walk on it or they find it difficult to do so. Such people either just sit still on the path, or keep thinking and planning without acting on it. During all this time of planning without any action, they are in a process of constant war with their conscience.

Adam, I don't know what I am writing. My thoughts are

random, unplanned. It seems that if I manage to hold one end of my thoughts, then the other one gets lost. Sometimes my mind wanders to one thing and sometimes to another.

Last night I prayed that I may see you in my dream. I dreamt about a family gathering in which I saw many people, but not you! One cannot even meet someone in dreams without Allah's (SWT) permission.

I took out your photo albums and saw your old pictures. I kept thinking, after you went away, how I collected all your pictures and pasted them in albums. My idea was to gather all your memories and keep them in albums. Now when I look at them, they all seem so meaningless to me and I feel that your real memories are in my heart preserved crystal clear and fresh, with no dust on them!

Memories are engraved on hearts. That is why people are able to spend all their lives just with the support of their memories.

Adam, you taught me a lot even after going away. Jazak'Allah Khair son.

Allah Hafiz.

Your Mother,
Urfana Ayub

Letter No 25.

The beauty of the Qur'an

Dearest son Adam Ayub .
Lots of love and prayers.

My child, my perception of you is like a fragrance, which I cannot confine to one place. I cannot see it or feel it, but I can perceive it all around me. It is difficult to explain. Maybe even you do not understand what I am trying to say.

Life is passing very swiftly. In my heart I have shared my feelings and incidents with you, and as a Muslim, I am very well aware of the fact that these letters will not reach you, Adam; neither can you hear what I am saying. But I do not want to lose the feeling, as if a sincere friend is there with whom I can share my innermost feelings.

I hope I can maintain this connection with you. This way you will always be like a companion in my life. I pray that nothing will come between this beautiful mother-son relationship. I wish it could remain intact forever and I may always be able to share my feelings and ideas with you.

I am changing! With each passing day this idea is getting firm in my mind. First I thought that people were changing. After giving a lot of thought to it, I have finally come to the conclusion that neither this world, nor its inhabitants or situations are changing. If anybody is changing, it's me, your mother, Adam!

There are two reasons for this change. First is the special blessing of Allah (SWT), which He bestowed upon me by connecting me with Qur'an. This connection had started before you went away. Meditation on Qur'an inclines one to learn lessons from daily situations.

As Allah (SWT) says in the Holy Qur'an:

"The Book We have sent down towards you which is full of Blessing, so that they might reflect upon its verses and that those of understanding may be reminded".

Surah Saad 38:29

The train of my heart was moving slowly. The scenes outside were gradually changing. But then came the second big reason for my change. It was your departure that speeded up my journey considerably. Now the train of my life, heart and mind is moving very swiftly. Even those scenes and stations where I want to slow down and enjoy are racing past against my will and I am simply left behind thinking.

Qur'an has lit a light in my heart whose radiance is so bright that it has dazzled my eyes. It is a vast ocean of knowledge of which I cannot assimilate even a few drops though I keep trying my entire life. I am amazed at what kind of world I was living in before. Sometimes, Adam, it seems as if I have recently converted to Islam. I don't know what sort of Islam I used to practise before. Probably this point differentiates a *"born and conventional Muslim"* from a *"volition and thinking one"*. Until now I was a conventional Muslim, just like so many other people who never think or

122

meditate about Islam and thus never become ideological Muslims.

To become a volitionl Muslim, it is mandatory to remove the rust of ignorance and neglect from our hearts. Our beloved Prophet (PBUH) said:

"These hearts get rusted just like iron gets rusted when water falls on it". He was asked, "O Rasool Allah (Messenger of Allah (SWT)) what will remove the rust from hearts?" He answered, "To remove the rust one must keep thinking of death repeatedly and secondly one should recite Qur'an".

(Mishkat)

Since I have started the quest for my religion, Praise be to Allah I have begun to understand it. It is my Allah's (SWT) benevolence that He gave me the guidance and ability to understand our religion before my death. I pray to Allah (SWT) to enable us all to comprehend Islam and make us meditate on it, Ameen.

In this world one often learns from one's mistakes. What worries me Adam is: why don't we learn from others' mistakes? There are so many examples around me that make me pray, *"O Lord please make these people learn something from the blunders and mistakes of others, so that they may be able to cleanse the dust of ignorance from their consciences".* The bare fact is that when we see someone bleeding, it may worry us a bit, but we actually feel the pain only when we bleed ourselves!

Allah (SWT) is extremely benevolent and merciful. He is never unjust to anyone; neither does He wish to be. He just sends small problems and losses our way so that we may correct ourselves. Unfortunately, people are so engrossed in the deceptions of this glamorous world that they completely neglect these little reminders from Allah (SWT) until He gives them a big jolt which makes them and the people around them start thinking. Alas, we have become so insensitive and immoral that neither do we understand, nor do we take any lesson from others' faults. May Allah (SWT) give guidance to us all (Ameen).

I never realised, Adam, that this letter has become so lengthy!

I leave you in Allah's (SWT) protection, my child. May Allah (SWT) give you a place in Jannat -ul- Firdous, may He make me meet you there and may He make your grave one of the many gardens of Heaven, Ameen. I pray that may your grave be spacious, airy and fragrant and may its window open in the gardens of paradise, Ameen.

Lots of love and prayers, Adam.

Your Mother, Urfana Ayub

Letter No 26.

Writing Therapy

My dear son Adam,

I miss you my child. Quite a few days have passed since I last wrote to you!

Writing letters to you is like a therapy for me. I had heard of *"writing therapy"*, where you put down your feelings on paper, but now I know that it is really effective and helps people a great deal. Talking to you makes me aware of the strong relationship which I share with you and also with the paper and pen. No one can understand this connection except Allah (SWT) and myself.

Adam, some peoples' attitudes confuse me. For instance a specific situation calls for merriment. One expects others to express their happiness on the occasion, but they do not behave accordingly. Maybe people do not know how to express happiness or else they are not happy for others.

Similarly, if it is a situation of sorrow for someone, then I feel we should sympathise with that person and try to feel his/her pain, but we do not often do so. I don't know why?

Why doesn't our ego allow us to appreciate someone's talent or praise him/her in appropriate words? Why Adam?

Why are we so narrow minded? What prevents us from participating in someone else's happiness, from

125

sympathising with others in grief, from expressing jubilation on someone's success?

Maybe it is jealousy, envy or simply being distressed at someone's success. At times I think that if unscrupulous people like us had any power over others we would not allow each other even a sip of water! Alhamdolilah, only Allah (SWT) has power over all this system!

I pray to Allah (SWT) to provide open-mindedness in our thinking and feelings, so that we can also enjoy other people's joy. Let us correct our attitudes so that we can feel others' grief and console them with kind and sympathetic words. Let other people's success make us happy. When our hearts and souls become sincere with others, and we find ourselves getting concerned for them as we do for our own selves, then Insha'Allah my Creator will grant all that to us which our hearts desire.

It is my firm belief, Adam, that when we sincerely wish well for others and are happy in their success; Allah (SWT) blesses us with similar joys and successes. The key factor here is a clean and pure heart, for Allah (SWT) knows very well what our hearts harbour. All the ugly deceit of heart is evident to Him. We can deceive the world, but we can never hide anything from Allah (SWT).

Sometimes we are very sincere with certain relatives. We deal with them with utmost honesty and love. But they reciprocate in a cold manner which hurts our soul. Then we start speculating that maybe there was some deficit in our attitude.

As a poet said:

I have no complaints against your behaviour, I swear
the scarcity might have been in my sincerity

Some people are never pleased with you no matter what you do for them. Even if you negate yourself and try to shape yourself according to their wishes in order to please them, still Adam, they remain bitter with you. No one is ever completely satisfied because thanklessness is intrinsic to our beings. I think that, even if someone sacrifices his life for another's happiness, an ungrateful person will still find fault with this sacrifice. We must take care not to break hearts by our attitudes, Adam, because when hearts are broken, they spread ill will for you, not well wishes.

As a poet said:

Do not bother if a mirror breaks
Hearts should not break as they are not sold in shops

Adam, it is true that we can buy many things from markets, but we can never mend broken hearts and relations. We must safeguard our character at all times.

As a poet said:

Protect your character from different seasons
For fragrance does not return to flower after leaving it

Adam, there are certain losses which we can never compensate for. Just like the scent emitted by flowers can never return to the blossom, I am also acutely aware that we spend our entire

127

lives trying to please other people and relatives. We even go as far as ignoring our own rights and selves. If we spent as much time, effort, sacrifice and love to build a relationship with Allah (SWT), and if we sincerely and wholeheartedly try to please Him, we will attain benefits beyond our expectations Insha'Allah. Our Sustainer will never let us down.

But alas! Our epicentre is still this world, its success and pleasures. As Allah's (SWT) people, we have forgotten to build a relationship with our Creator. Yet Adam, by this I do not mean that we should totally ignore this world and not care about other people's rights. Allah (SWT) stresses upon us to maintain relations. Undoubtedly we must ensure a high standard in maintaining ties with others. Every relationship demands its rights. Parents have their own rights, so too siblings, children, spouses, friends, companions, relatives, Muslims and non-Muslims. Everyone has their rights, which we must fulfil.

But I am talking about those unjust relationships and attitudes, which in trying to satisfy, we ignore the rights of our Creator and Sustainer.

Adam, our behaviour must be moderate in all aspects, because Allah (SWT) is pleased by moderation and has ordered us to maintain it in all our dealings. We cannot please everybody at all times. We can only honour the rights of all our relationships according to Allah's (SWT) orders and the Holy Prophet's (PBUH) teachings, then leave the rest to Allah (SWT).

Another thing which I have learnt from life is that the sentiments of our heart are in Allah's (SWT) control. We cannot change anyone's thinking; neither can we inculcate our love in someone else's heart no matter how much we pray for it. Our hearts are in the control of our Lord only. Allah (SWT) says in the Holy Qur'an:

"And He has united their hearts. If you had given away all the riches of the earth, you could not have so united them, but Allah has united them. Certainly He is Almighty, All Wise."

Surah Al-Anfal (The Spoils of War), 8:63

Patience, respect and being helpful to people are those qualities which can soften and mould the toughest of the hearts, but only if Allah (SWT) so desires. At times Adam, it seems as if man is inherently weak, so when he respects others or does work for them, he expects appreciation and encouragement in return, as he considers that as his wage. But we must pin all our hopes and expectations onto our Master only. He will repay all our endeavours in the best possible way. Building up our hopes around people will only injure us with their sharp prickles and cause repeated heartbreak. Man is so stupid and obstinate that he keeps on nurturing expectations from others. All our anticipations must be directed towards our Creator only, and our attitude while carrying out any good deeds or gestures must be to do good and forget about it.

Allah Hafiz.

Your Mother, Urfana Ayub

129

Letter No 27.

Iqra (Read)

Dear son Adam,
Peace be upon you.

I want to share some good news with you. For some time I have been thinking that I must learn the correct pronunciation *(Tajweed)* of Qur'an. The word Tajweed literally means *"to make something better or to improve"*. The study of Tajweed means that each word and letter within Qur'an is taught to be recited in the proper way, right from its source with all its associated properties *(Makhraj)*.

A girl living close to our house has completed the course of *Aalima* (scholarship) and has started to teach women at her residence. I went there yesterday. There were a few other women present. Our teacher kindly handed us the booklets used by other students (children) whom she also teaches, so that we could start our lessons right away and later buy our own booklets. Adam, when I opened my booklet, there on the first page was your name written in English. That booklet belonged to some other mother's Adam. Tears came to my eyes. I thanked Allah (SWT) and began my lessons.

What a coincidence it was! Out of so many booklets I received the one which had your name written on it. Though it seemed a chance happening, in reality there was Allah's (SWT) wisdom hidden in it. He keeps reminding us time and again, Alhamdolilah.

I heartily pray to Allah (SWT) that I may be able to learn the correct recitation of Qur'an. We find time to do all the chores of this world, but we do not find time to study our religion. The one who recites Qur'an correctly will enjoy a high status in the hereafter, as evident from the words of RasoolAllah, The messenger of Allah (SWT):

"On the day of resurrection the reciter of Qur'an would be told 'recite the verses of Qur'an in the same magnificent voice and manner in which you used to recite them in the world. Recitation of each verse will exalt you one level higher. Your destination will be near where the last verse that you recite will take you'."

(Tirmidhi)

This is a book whose first revelation began with a command, Iqra meaning *"read"*. Today most of the people who believe in this book are ignorant about its sayings. It is read traditionally at marriages and funerals. Most people of the muslim ummah either do not pronounce its words correctly, nor do they know its meanings. How can our destiny be guidance from Qur'an in such a scenario?

There are many supplications to ask for Allah's (SWT) help regarding the understanding of Qur'an. Out of these I particularly like Hadrat Umar's (RA) prayer:

"O Allah (SWT) make me understand and meditate on, whatever my tongue recites from this book (Qur'an) and let me comprehend its meaning and wonders. Let me act according to its sayings while I am alive. Verily you have

control over anything."

May Allah (SWT) grant us the ability to understand our religion, teach it to others and act on it, Ameen.

My child may you be in Allah's (SWT) protection.

Your Mother,
Urfana Ayub

Letter No 28:

What is Shirk?

Dear son Adam Ayub,
Lots of love and prayers.

Today, I am very upset. When I glanced at the front page of an Urdu newspaper, there was an advertisement for a *Bangali Baba* on the front page, and the second page boasted about the expertise of a skilled sorceress. Both these advertisements plunged me into a sea of thoughts.

Is this not Shirk? (Polytheism)
If this is not Shirk then what else is?
Do we know what Shirk is?

I feel that Shirk is increasing with time. We are openly involved in Shirk. These *Aamils, sorcerers, Bangali Babas, Mr. Taubah, Peers* (self appointed saints) and the rest of their lot Nauozobillah claim to have those powers, might, control and qualities which we ascribe to Allah (SWT) only.

They offer a solution to every problem: to destroy someone's life with magic, cures for illness, success in exams. In short, whatever you wish for, whatever the issue. These people will solve them *"just with eleven Tasbeehat"* (recitation of certain words for so many number of times). They promise to ensure riches, love and fame for everyone. They claim the knowledge even to break stones apart. No problem is too great or small: your beloved will succumb to you, magic spells will be removed, a new husband or admirer will be yours within

24 hours, all obstacles to your business will be lifted, your children will be obedient, immigration problems will be solved, childlessness or infant mortality will be worries of the past. Services even cover getting married, preventing a marriage, winning prizes and lotteries (especially Euro and Lotto), protection against the ill will of Sautan (husband's second wife) and overcoming disappointment in love or friendships. For all the above issues, one thousand percent guarantee of success.

I have heard many real life stories where young girls and women have been sexually abused by these so called Amils and people claiming to represent religion. These individuals are targeting vulnerable people in vulnerable situations. I feel that innocent members of the society males and females included cannot see the real faces and agenda (financial benefit) behind their service. I have heard people saying they don't charge any money, we want to give them as a good will gesture. The Amils say that they have no cost for providing their services and they only want to benefit humanity. At the same time they make their clients feel inclined to pay them money. A true servant of Allah should not be taking a single penny or any worldly benefit for his services.

There are so many types of Shirk which we do not acknowledge as Shirk. The truth is; man is weakened by the problems or tests which he is subjected to, which is quite understandable. Allah (SWT) tests His people to see what their reaction will be in difficult times. I feel as if Allah (SWT) tries out the Imaan of His people. Adam, when you went away from this world, I also felt as if Allah (SWT) was testing me to see what would be the response of a mother who lost her beloved teenage son. Will she complain or be patient?

As soon as man succumbs to trying circumstances, then Satan takes over and opens satanic doors to that person. These evil doors come in different forms. For instance, the unfortunate man begins to take help from the Aamils and Peers instead of relying on Allah (SWT). People go to the shrines of Peers and seek assistance from those who, oblivious to this world, are buried there. They ask for fulfilment of their needs and desires on these shrines and put decorative cloths on the graves of Peers in order to please them. They completely forget that only Allah (SWT) is our real Master and Sustainer and He is present here in this world very close to us. He knows what goes on in our hearts; our every problem and sorrow is evident to him. We just need to call out for His help with a sincere heart and pure emotions. He will Insha'Allah listen to our problems, but alas we have more faith in these false beliefs than in our Sustainer.

As a poet said:

You have expectations from idols and are disappointed in Allah
Tell me what else is Kaafari (being a non-Muslim)

Some people are in the habit of determining a Faal (a method of predicting the future). These people place total faith in the writings on cards which are picked up by a parrot/bird. They believe that whatever is written on these cards is destined to happen. Anyone who believes in astrology or any other means of predicting the future becomes subservient to these practices. Some people go after amulets and magic and thus lose their Imaan. We are doing so many things except one, which is absolutely essential, that is: pure, complete and unconditional obedience and trust in Allah (SWT).

We recite Kalimah daily and admit that *"there is no Allah beside Allah (SWT) and Muhammad (PBUH) is Allah's (SWT) messenger"*, but in practical matters, we are obedient to Shirk.

Apart from parrots and cards that foretell our future, there are many other misconceptions prevalent in our society. These include taking specific dates and numbers as unlucky, or regarding as bad omens such things as a black cat crossing one's path, a crow cawing, the twitching of the left or right eye, spilling of milk or sugar, the breaking of a mirror and many other superstitions.

Adam, what can I say about other people? I myself used to read the column *"How your week would be"* in my days of ignorance. I am thankful to my Creator that He gave me an understanding of our religion and pulled me out of my incomprehension.

People who keenly read or hear radio programs predicting how their week will turn out are also involved in a type of Shirk. There are so many varieties of Shirk that it has become difficult to identify it.

The Qur'an teaches us that, except Allah, nobody knows what is going to happen the next moment or tomorrow, because it is knowledge of *Ghaib* (the unseen). If someone claims to have knowledge about the *Ghaib*, it cannot be true, because he only knows what Allah (SWT) has given to him.

Allah says in the holy Qur'an:

Say *"I hold not for myself [the power of] benefit or harm, except what Allah has willed. If I had knowledge of the unseen, I should have gathered ample good, and no harm should have touched me: I am but a warner, and a bringer of glad tidings to those who have faith."*

Surah Al-A'raf (The Heights), 7:188

Our beloved Prophet Muhammad (PBUH) had access only to that much knowledge of the Ghaib which Allah (SWT) had granted him. If he had full knowledge of the Ghaib, he would have averted many losses by taking preventive measures against them. If Allah's messenger had no control over his profits and losses, then how can these so-called Peers and Aalims claim to control their own or someone else's successes and failures.

From now on I will be very vigilant that I may not do the following!

- Ask from someone other than Allah
- Go to shrines of holy people and ask for their help
- Make Peers a means to gain access to Allah (SWT)
- Equate holy/knowledgeable people to Allah in respect
- Equate Holy Prophet's (PBUH) status to Allah
- Take out the Faal (divination)
- Believe in omens
- Believe in astrology or seek advice from a fortune-teller.
- Make people ask for guidance from Allah on my behalf

I remember, Adam, in my childhood I had a chance to see a few shrines of holy people in Pakistan. Alhamdulilah, Allah (SWT) had given guidance to Nana Abbu and Nani Ammi not to be part of any Shirk, but we visited a few shrines in Karachi purely out of respect. When insight came regarding these

137

things we simply stopped going.

Your sister often asked me what shrines look like. I took her to one just for the sake of teaching her. I went to such a place after a very long time and I saw people involved in different types of activities based on Shirk. The outskirts of the shrine presented a picture of a funfair with stalls selling flowers, garlands, decorative sheets, scented sticks and other things.

People had placed small cribs in a room. I've heard that people donate these as well. Maybe they do it to have children? May Allah pardon us, show us the way to true guidance and keep us away from Shirk (Ameen).

Adam, I was talking to someone on this topic today. She told me that in their family, when they want to make any major decision or plan to do something, first of all they seek permission from their Peer sahib whether that particular thing should be done or not? After that, they pray to Allah (SWT) for it and ask for His guidance. I wonder how people could be so deaf, dumb and blind. Don't they have any sense at all? They never try to reason things out. They only follow others blindly.

Adam, if uneducated people do such seemingly ignorant actions, one can understand that this is because their minds have not been enlightened by knowledge. But it is beyond any logic when educated, knowledgeable and intelligent people also have the same perspective.

However, even if we are not involved in Shirk, then we can still be slaves of our self-interest. We do what we want to whether it is right or wrong.

None of us admits that being a slave of ego is a form of Shirk. People will naturally claim that they are not involved in Shirk. Because according to them, Shirk means worshipping idols only and they are not doing any such thing. All the rest is permitted. I pray that may Allah protect us from this great sin and give us the insight to identify Shirk (Ameen).

Adam, please do not misunderstand me, dear son. I deeply respect all our religious scholars and Aalims. Even the fish in the oceans pray for people who gain knowledge of their religion and then teach it to others. If Allah (SWT) has exalted them in their position, who are we to undermine them? We may call these people Islamic scholars, Peers, Wali Allah (friends of Allah), Buzurg or any other name. They are well respected in society, which is quite understandable, but at no time should this respect ever change to Shirk! We some-times do not even notice this dangerous transition of our actions from respect to Shirk.

Adam, I think that the best and easiest way to judge these people is to find out who these religious Aalims are trying to connect us with; Allah or their own selves? When we associate with them we respect them and at times elevate their status to that of, Nauzobillah, Allah or His Messenger (PBUH). When we start following them, we tend to push Allah's orders to the back and give more importance to their sayings. Anybody who claims religious authority in the name of Allah (SWT) and His Messenger (PBUH) should be practising the basic obligatory (fard) acts of worship i.e. oneness of Allah (Tauheed), Salah (prayer) 5 times a days, Fasting, paying Zakah and performing Hajj. I feel that any individual who follows any person who doesn't practice themselves the basic 5 pillars of Islam and encourage the followers, are taking the easy path. This is definitely Shirk, Adam!

We need to beware of dangerous people who themselves are blinded by greed, worldly glamour and luxuries, and under the pretence of religious Aalims, urge us to defy Allah's (SWT) commandments.

The Qur'an also warns true believers about the tactics of so-called Aalims and scholars of Ahle Kitab (People using scriptures, meaning followers of the Bible and Taurah):

"O you who have attained to faith! Behold many of the rabbis and monks do indeed wrongfully devour men's possessions and bar them away from the path of Allah. But as for all who hoard up treasures of gold and silver and do not spend them for the sake of Allah- give them the tiding of grievous suffering."

Surah At-Taubah (The Repentance), 9:34

There are many examples in our society where we have ascribed qualities and characteristics to people which belong only to our Master. We must think about all those wrong (Shirkia) names we give to these people like: *Daata* (giver), *Ghaus al Azam* (the greatest listener of problems), *Ganj Bakhsh* (bestower of treasure), *Mushkil Kusha* (the solver of all problems), *Dastgir* (Persian, literally meaning one who holds someone's hand, referring to one who gets someone out of trouble), *Ghareeb Nawaz* (one who grants (bounties) to the poor) etc. These are purely qualities of our Sustainer only, not of any human being.

"Those you worship besides Him are nothing but mere names which you and your forefathers have invented, for which Allah has revealed no sanction."

Surah Yusuf (Prophet Joseph), 12:40

Adam, Ghaus al Azam means *"the greatest listener of problems"*. This quality can only be attributed to Allah (SWT). How can we ever call a person by this name, no matter how pious or knowledgeable he is? No doubt they were a pious person and a true servant of Allah.

Our Master says in the holy Qur'an:

"Who listens to the destitute when it calls on Him, and relieves his suffering, and makes you inheritors of the earth? Is there another Allah besides Allah? Little it is that you heed!"

Surah An-Naml (The Ants), 27:62

Similarly, Ghareeb Nawaz means *"one who grants (bounties) to the poor"*. Again, this is a quality which is attributable to Allah (SWT) and Him only.

As Allah (SWT) says in Holy Qur'an:

"O mankind, you are all those in need of Allah, while Allah is the one Free of need, the Praiseworthy."

Surah Al-Fatir (The Originator), 35:15

Then Adam, Mushkil Kusha means "the solver of all problems". We cannot ascribe this quality to any of Allah's messengers or the companions of messengers. Not even to our beloved Prophet Muhammad (PBUH) so loved by Allah (SWT) Himself. This is a characteristic of our Sustainer only, not of anyone else.

"If Allah touches you with harm, there is no remover of it but He, and if He touches you with good, then He is Capable of doing everything."

Surah Al-An'am (The Cattle), 6:17

Adam, I grew up listening to these names without realising that I am engulfed by Shirk. But now alhamdolilah I understand that *Ganj Bakhsh, "Bestower of Treasure"*, is none other than Allah (SWT).

"Allah (SWT) provides sustenance to whom He pleases without measure."

Surah Ale-Imran (The Family of Imran), 3:37

"And that it is He who enriches and suffices."

Surah An-Najm (The Star), 53:48

Our last Prophet Muhammad (PBUH) said, *"Allah (SWT) would ask the person exposed to the least of the tortures of hell, 'If you had a world full of riches at this time, would you give it to save yourself from torture?' He would say 'Yes this is my desire' and Allah (SWT) would say 'When you were in the world of spirits, I had asked for a much smaller demand which was not to ascribe any partner with Me but you did not pay heed and continued practicing Shirk'."*

(Sahih Bukhari)

Adam, the following is a Hindu's complaint which provides food for thought for all Muslims:

"I go to temple, you go to shrines. I eat prasaad (Hindi word roughly equivalent to Sacrament) you eat tabarrak (literally means something blessed, but a term also used for rough equivalent to Sacrament). I present coconut to Allahs; you present decorative sheets to your Buzurgs. I get Aasheervaad (blessings); you get your murad (desire). I join both my hands before my Allah (idol); you prostrate at the shrines. My difficulties are eased and you also get what you asked for. When there is no difference between you and me; then why are our Allahs are different? Your Prophet used to go to Mosque; then why do you go to shrines? Your Prophet used to raise his arms in supplication; why do you embrace the graves? Your Prophet asked only from Allah (SWT); why do you bother with shrines and shrine holders? Just tell me if I am a Kafir (non believer), what are you then?"

May you be in Allah's (SWT) protection my child

Your Mother,
Urfana Ayub

My supplication

My very dear son Adam Ayub,
Peace be upon you.
Lots of prayers and love.

Today someone sent me a poem which actually is a Dua and I liked it very much. I want to share this Dua with you and pray that Allah fulfils it for every Muslim, Ameen.

Neither control, nor glory, just give me the ability
To follow the path which leads to You and be an example for this world
May Your blessings be on me, may I be rewarded for my toils
Let me not lust after the worldly wealth, let me earn fair and square
Let my mind be filled by You, let my breath be scented by You.
Let your fear salvage me, rid me of all the other fears
Day and night I pray to You O Lord
You are Merciful, You are generous, please get me out of all my troubles

(Ameen)

Adam, our biggest accomplishment should be that Allah (SWT) shows us the right path, which leads us to Him and gives us the ability to remain steadfast on that path. Lust for this world has blinded us all, including me. All the chores of this world, its possessions and riches have misguided man so much that he has forgotten why he came into the world? So why did Allah (SWT) create him?

If we do not forget the purpose of our creation and only desire that much wealth that we can earn by fair means, our lives could be very different. If only that would happen! The other problem with man is that, despite knowing the truth and having insight, he continues to displease Allah (SWT) out of fear of other people and wondering, *"what will others say?"* We totally forget that by displeasing our Creator, we will never be able to please His creation. But man is ungrateful and his desires are never satiated. Even if he has the whole world at his disposal, he would still be unhappy. Rather than being grateful, he would desire one more world. I pray that our minds become free of the fear of this world and its inhabitants and we should only fear Allah (SWT), Ameen. Sometimes I feel that, *Nauzobillah*, our relationship with Allah (SWT) is based on fear and compulsion.

> *Prostration for His love will make worship a pleasure*
> *There is nothing but this world in empty bows*
> *They say that we just have to fulfil our duty*
> *Seems like they are repaying their debts to the Creator*
> *Don't let your bows make you a disbeliever*
> *You bow in one place and think of another*

The fact is, Adam, that for most people, including me, the act of prostration is just an empty gesture which is filled by the thoughts of this world. During the whole of Salah we keep thinking about *"what am I going to cook, what will I wear, what did somebody say to me, what will I do tomorrow"*, etc. We offer Salah as if we had borrowed something from Allah (SWT). The way we hastily do so looks like we are eager to repay a debt, where our hearts are devoid of any gratitude for the blessings of the Benefactor. We all know that Salah should be an indispensable part of the life of a Muslim. That is why the first question in the hereafter regarding the fulfilment of Fardh (essentials) will be about Salah.

As Allah (SWT) says in Qur'an:

"And be steadfast in Salah and give Zakah and bow down with those who bow down".

Surah Al-Baqarah (The Cow), 2:43

A Hadith of the Holy Prophet (PBUH) states,

"Salah is as much important for the religion as it is the head for the body"
Sahih Bukhari

It is my heartiest prayer that every Muslim should offer the Salah regularly and with full concentration and submission, Ameen.

I plead to Allah (SWT) that when I bow down before Him it should be purely for Him. When I stand up for Namaz, I should only be thinking about my Master and not about this deceptive world. I should only be thinking about my Creator Who is with me from my beginning (from an insignificant drop of water) till my very end (my repose in the grave), who never ever forgets me. Yet even during the Namaz, I cannot think purely of Him. Adam, I pray to Allah (SWT) that I get *"quality"*, or in other words, concentration and submission in my Namaz, Ameen.

I pray that Allah (SWT) may design us the way He likes. Lead us to the right path and give us the best of the abilities to act accordingly, Ameen.

Leaving you in Allah's (SWT) protection.

Your Mother,
Urfana Ayub

Letter No 30.

Sadqa e Jariya

My dear son Adam Ayub,
Peace be upon you.
Lots of love and prayers.

Every time I start writing a letter to you, I feel like asking, *"How are you?"* then I realise that this letter is not going to reach you. I am sure you are well and in the protection of my Creator.

Yesterday Baba and Daddy went to Saudi Arabia to perform Umrah. From there they will go to Pakistan. They telephoned me today with the news that they have performed Umrah, praise be to Allah I pray to Allah (SWT) to accept their Umrah and other prayers and let us have the opportunity and honour to go there too.

Adam, I gave a list of Duas to Daddy in which I mentioned special prayers for my children. Some of these were collective prayers, like prayer for faith (Imaan), long life and health. Instinctively I wrote these Duas against your name as well. Then I realised that you do not need health or long life in your journey. You only need prayers and Sadaqa e Jariya (eternal reward)!

It is so strange, Adam, that when a person is alive he does not even think of making preparations for the next life, but when the candle of life is about to blow out, one starts worrying about what will happen in the hereafter.

148

When children go for their driving tests, mothers are so worried about them and keep praying that the children do not get confused and remain confident and succeed. Mothers do not rest easy until the child comes home with the result. Imagine how important this small success in her child's worldly life is for the mother! She is worried about his or her failure.

But have we ever asked ourselves honestly whether we worry that much when our child does not offer Salah, when he is ignorant of Allah's (SWT) commands and our Prophet's ways of life (Sunnah)? When the child is not living his life according to our religion; the life which can end at any moment? Do we ever lie awake at night fearing for the child's failure in the hereafter? The eternal success and failure that will be never-ending, with no chance to re-take the test.

We do not understand this point. I realised and understood many things after you departed from this world. It was like waking from a deep sleep. May Allah (SWT) keep me *"awake"* for the rest of my life, Ameen.

I have wandered far away from my point, Adam. I was telling you about Baba and Daddy's Umrah. Do you remember when you went for Umrah with Baba and then visited Pakistan after that? I still remember that when you returned from your journey, your health had improved so much Masha Allah that I did not recognise you. You always loved going to Pakistan. You loved its climate, meeting your Nana, Nani, Mamoons, Mumanis and other relatives.

Daddy will pray for your success in the Hereafter. All the

charity work that has been done on your behalf after you; may Allah (SWT) accept it and spread its benefits, Ameen.

I have also understood the meaning of Sadaqa e Jariya since your passing. This refers to all those actions which bring reward to the deceased. The benefits of such good deeds are long-lasting; for example, having a well dug for people's water needs, or a shelter built to provide comfort, planting trees, ensuring a healthy environment with fresh air, donating wheelchairs or other necessary equipment to a hospital, or catering for the educational needs of a deserving student, and many other good deeds that continue to provide benefits over the long term.

Now I know why every one of us must try to participate in all these activities which bring long lasting rewards. The reason is - we do not know whether anyone will perform any good deed on our behalf after our death or not.

You are very lucky, Adam, because your parents, grandparents, Phuphie and other family members are engaged in works of Sadaqa e Jariya on your behalf. Not all deceased people are that lucky to have so many relatives working for them. Usually people leave behind their children after their death, but it is not always the case that the children will worry about collecting reward for their parents. The brutal reality of life is that in this world, man lives with utmost selfishness and vanity, with little regard for family members. After someone dies, his/her relatives are more interested and worried about getting their share of the inheritance, rather than doing anything for Sadaqa e Jariya for the dead person. I have seen family relationships breaking up on such occasions.

Now I try to take some money out of what we keep saving to spend on our homes, family and business and deposit it with Allah (SWT) for my own sake. By doing so I may have some satisfaction of eternal reward.

Hadhrat Umar (RA) quotes our beloved Prophet (PBUH) as saying,

"If you rely on Allah (SWT) the way you should rely on Him, then He will give sustenance to you as He gives to birds that set out of their nests hungry in the mornings and return to their homes with full stomach in the evenings"

Tirmidhi.

I felt ashamed after reading this Hadith. Don't I have even as much trust in Allah (SWT) as these birds do!

It has been snowing for several days. I have stocked up on all sorts of provisions so that there are sufficient essential household items. Though a car is always available and I go out almost daily, still I stocked up as a safety measure. There is a particular spot outside the window where I put food for the birds. Today when I glanced at that spot, it reminded me of that Hadith. The pieces of bread were buried under snow, and small birds were pecking at them by inserting their beaks under the snow.

I thought: our Sustainer has provided food for the birds even in this extreme weather. On the other hand, here am I, with my central heating, a car outside for all my errands, money in my purse, and everything I could possibly need; yet my level of trust in Allah (SWT) cannot match that of these tiny birds.

This morning when I was going to drop Ahmad to school, I saw flocks of birds in the sky. The thought struck me, *"Where will these birds find their food today as everything is covered with snow?"* But even birds get their stomachs filled before sleeping.

Masha'Allah different shades of Allah's (SWT) powers are spread all around us. It is up to us now what we see in these signs, what we learn and what we do!

I am forced to think that Allah (SWT) is inviting us to meditate on His signs. How He gives life to the barren land and makes different plants grow there for people and animals. Have we ever really pondered on these growing flowers, vegetables and fruits? How Allah (SWT) makes a plant grow from a lifeless seed by His power. Then He adorns these plants with delicious fruits and vegetables of different colours. Every fruit has its own beautiful colour, shape and unique fragrance. On top of it each one is so delicious and full of nutrition.

All this vegetation is produced by the earth, which is under the control of Allah (SWT). The same earth which we walk upon with pride and power, without paying heed to the fact that we were created from earth, we fill our stomachs with the produce of this earth and to this earth we shall return after our death.

I am extremely impressed by the way each plant has its own seed, flavour, colour, shape, fragrance and qualities, which are entirely different from other plants, although all were irrigated from the same water.

Unfortunately, no one has the time to think about these things. If we want to maintain a relationship with Allah (SWT), we must pay attention to His many signs which are spread all around us in the universe; like rain, water, vegetables, fruits, flowers, trees, their shape and scent; different animals and so many of His other creations. If we want to get close to Allah (SWT) then, even while cutting fruits and vegetables for our meals, we need to think about His signs for a couple of minutes.

Adam, every fruit is prepared and packed in Allah's (SWT) factory. The skin of a banana protects it. While the other fruits and nuts like oranges, apples, walnuts, almonds, pistachios and coconuts also reach us in full covering and protection. Even each grain of rice has its own delicate outer casing. Not only this, Allah's (SWT) magnificent power and might arranges for the supreme development and growth of a human foetus inside its mother's womb within three "dark zones".

"He created you all from one soul. Then He made from it its mate, and He sends down for you from the grazing livestock eight mates. He creates you in the wombs of your mothers, creation after creation, within three dark zones. That is Allah, your Lord; to Him belongs dominion. There is no deity except Him, so how are you turned away?"

Surah Az-Zumar (The Groups), 39:6

The three dark zones refer to: 1. Abdominal wall of mother, 2. The womb, 3. Membranes encasing the foetus. If He provides food to the baby within its mother's womb, where even the mother has no access to the baby and the growing foetus is purely and completely dependent on Allah (SWT), so would He not provide sustenance to an adult, intelligent and complete human being later on?

There are countless examples of Allah's (SWT) benevolence and might which are the best of proof of Allah's (SWT) oneness. All these examples are spread before us. If, in spite of all this, we do not listen and act according to His commands, then tell me, who is to blame? That is why Allah (SWT) repeatedly says in the Holy Qur'an that these things are for those who have sense! Senseless and ignorant people will not be able to see them even after looking at them; they will not hear the truth even after listening to it.

I pray to Allah (SWT) to let us identify the truth in this world so that we can improve our hereafter, Ameen.
Allah (SWT) says in the Holy Qur'an:

"Indeed, in the creation of the heavens and the earth and the alternation of the night and the day are signs for those who understand, to remember Allah (SWT) while standing or sitting or [lying] on their sides and give thought to the creation of the heavens and the earth, [saying], 'Our Lord, You did not create this aimlessly; exalted are You; then protect us from the punishment of the Fire'."

Surah Ale-Imran (The Family of Imran), 3:191-192

May you be in Allah's (SWT) protection my child.

Your Mother, Urfana Ayub

154

Letter No 31.

Who are we?

Dear son Adam Ayub,
Peace be upon you, Lots of love and prayers.

Your mother misses you a lot; especially so when I meet new people and they ask me about my children and their ages. As usual I still count you as my child and you are growing in the world of my heart with each passing year. In Sha Allah on 7th May you will become 24 years old.

Adam, yesterday I was having a phone conversation. When we are worried or tense we at once tend to turn to other people for help. We completely forget that we are all beggars before Allah (SWT), and one beggar cannot give anything to another beggar because he does not have anything to give. Only a king can fulfil the beggar's needs and our king is only our Sustainer, our Helper; our Allah Ta'ala.

Allah (SWT) always waits for us with open doors looking out for when his people will return to him. But what do we do? We phone tens of people to ask for their help. At times, we get the engaged signal. But Allah's (SWT) line is always available and never engaged or busy for His people. Unfortunately, we do not often use this line. Perhaps man is not satisfied until he makes a few phone calls and tells other people his troubles. Instead of turning to people, if someone sits on a prayer mat and talks with his Creator, then He will definitely listen, as He knows all our worries too. What's more, Allah (SWT) has the power and ability to fulfil all of man's desires Subhan'Allah (Glory be to Allah).

Adam, whenever I listen to this Hamd of Abrar ul Haque's, I wonder where we have become lost and why we have forgotten ourselves?

Your colours your shades
Oh, Allah your colours your shades
They're everywhere, no matter where I go in this world
Your signs are with me everywhere
You granted me and I forgot
You granted again, but I did not thank
I changed the course of rivers
I learnt to fly in the air
My destinations are the stars
Still I need your help
I am entangled in races and strata
My heart is covered with the dust which blurs the truth
How can I complain about my body, but even my spirit is not eager
What to talk of following your commands, I even do not
remember to mention You anymore
O Lord let my spirit at least fight my body
O Bulleh Shah we are not going to die, it is someone else who is
buried in the grave.
Neither am I a believer who goes to the mosque, nor do I follow
the practices of a non-believer.
Neither am I a pure one nor am I among the impure,
I am neither Musa (Moses) nor Fir'aun (Pharaoh)
O Bulleh Shah I know not who I am?

Adam, we are divided into so many sects. People of one group do not consider the people of another group as Muslim. Every person claims to belong to the best of sects. Muslims do not hesitate to call each other non-Muslims. People of the entire world are fighting with each other and dying. In

156

the five years since your departure Adam, this world has become a worse place to live. Muslims hate other Muslims to the extent of killing them. Murder and war is rampant. People are slaughtering other humans like animals.

One day I was watching a news channel where they were showing an innocent man whose tongue was cut off by another man just for the sake of money. Adam I cried bitterly that day knowing that brute did not even consider he was not cutting a cloth or vegetable; he was cutting another person's tongue! We all claim to belong to a religion which does not allow us to behave with such brutality, even to enemies. But when I saw that footage, my soul was wounded and I cried out in horror. I could not sleep that night. Is our conscience completely dead? On the face of it, we are alive, but the feeling of guilt is dead in us. As someone said it so well,

When spirit leaves the body, people grieve and mourn
Why doesn't any one cry when the character dies?

I feel like telling these wild beasts, *"Your consciences are dead; you are like living corpses which are walking about."* A few bad people in our society spoil the good name and reputation for the rest of us Muslims. We Muslims might declare other Muslims as Kafirs, but only Kafirs (the non-Muslim) call us all Muslims (whether good or bad). This is food for thought for all of us, Adam!

Allah Hafiz dear son. I leave you in the protection of Allah (SWT).

Your Mother, Urfana Ayub

157

Letter No 32.

Humanitarianism

My dear son Adam Ayub,
Peace be upon you.
Your mother sends you her sincere prayers and love.

I want to talk to you, but I do not know what to say. It has started snowing again since yesterday. Early this morning we received a message from Ahmad's school notifying us that it would be closed today due to bad weather. Last week also the school shut for one day due to heavy snowfall.

Adam, whenever it snows, my heart gets depressed and remains so until the snow melts completely. One reason for this is that you went away from us in this weather. The memory of your departure freezes the world of my heart. When I saw your grave for the first time it was covered with snow.

I also feel that snow disrupts our lives. Yesterday it took me two and a half hours to reach home from my office, although the snowfall had just begun at that time. There was a traffic jam because everyone was in a hurry to get home.

Forget it Adam, what am I talking about? Interestingly, for the first time in my life I keenly observed and concentrated on the snowflakes and the hail. When soft snowflakes fall, it seems as if pieces of cotton wool are drifting down from the sky. They melt the instant they land. It is beautiful to see them softly falling to earth. When hail falls, you expect the pellets of ice to make a sound, since they are travelling

158

very fast and from quite a distance. This makes you think of the all-encompassing power of Allah (SWT).

As a poet said:

Oh Allah, Oh Allah
Whoever made an effort
Finally, did find you
You are everyone's guide
Oh, Allah O Allah
This earth, sky and beyond them
All the worlds reflect You
The dawn spreads in a new way
Grass and flowers grow on boulders
There is a world living in each star
The moon and sun reflect your light
Oh, Allah Oh Allah
Whoever made an effort
Finally, did find you
You are everyone's guide
Oh, Allah Oh Allah

Allah (SWT) says in the holy Qur'an:

"Say to them, 'Observe what is in the heavens and earth but of no avail will be signs or warners to the people who do not believe'."

Surah Yunus (Prophet Jonah), 10:10.

Adam, Daddy and Baba have still not returned from Umrah. They sent a text message today telling me that they are in Madinah. They told me that construction work is going on

159

around the Khana Kaa'ba (holy mosque in Makkah) to increase its capacity. This will help more people can be accommodated for Hajj and Umrah. Every year there is an increase in number of people who go to perform Hajj and Umrah. Therefore, there is an immense gathering there. Adam, though you left this world at a very tender age, I am very happy that Allah (SWT) gave you a chance to see Khana Ka'aba and perform Umrah and other prayers there, praise be to Allah.

Adam, when you left us, Facebook was the most popular tool of social interaction. Now it has changed by leaps and bounds. The boundaries have diminished. Now you can make a free call or send messages to any country around the globe via WhatsApp, Line, Viber and many more such servies. Thanks to this technology, I recently got in touch with an old school and college friend after 24 years. It made me very happy. Old friendships are so beautiful. They readily reconnect whenever you want to get back in touch. Any intervening gap vanishes quickly. With these relationships of the heart, sincere friends, close relatives, and even some strangers, stay close to your heart even though they are miles apart. Twenty-four years seems a very long period, but if there is sincerity, love and feelings for the other person, distances don't matter. That is why Allah (SWT) has made human relations superior to all others. To be good to every person is the basic rule of humanitarianism.

When one is distant from family and friends, their memories remain with us as companions. No matter how many years pass since you last met them, the memories are enough to provide comfort and support for the rest of our lives.

Often when one loses hope of ever seeing loved ones again, the memories remain a valuable possession to treasure.

I miss your smile and things you used to say very much. I am always aware of the fact that you used to live in our house. You are part of my being. I have collected all your belongings which you left behind and formed a "box of memories" with them. Your first teddy bear given to you on you first birthday by your Phuphie and Chachcha's is now in my room. Likewise, there are many other things we associate with your memories. They are present amidst us even today and will always remain so.

One day somebody asked *"What is the difference between promises and memories?"* The answer: *"Man breaks promises and memories break the man".*

Adam, I met a lady whose son had died. She told me that they have preserved their son's room exactly like it was in his life. She has locked the room and nobody is allowed to touch the things present there. She feels that the room, its things and their arrangement remind her of her son.

In contrast, Adam, except for a few items, I have distributed most of your things to other people. When you went away, initially I wanted to preserve each and every thing which was connected with you. If anybody had your photograph, I took it from them. Your writings, your college and university work; I safely put away all the things which were related to you. I felt comforted by this, but as time passed, I realised that these things mean nothing. I do not need to open a photo album to look at your photographs. I do not need to take your belongings out of your cupboard and feel them. I

161

don't have to bring out your passport to convince myself that you actually lived in this world, because you are living in my heart. Indeed, you are alive and growing with each passing year.

When a person finds abode in someone's heart, then all other things become insignificant. You are a lucky boy, Adam! You not only live in the hearts of your parents and siblings, but also in hearts of many other relatives. Before you had just one "home". Now, thanks to *Taray Janay Kay Baad*, you dwell even in those homes with which you have no blood connection.

People often tell me, *"Adam's book is lying on my side table and I read it time and again"*. All these people remember you by name and also pray for you.

In Pakistan Nani Jan is actively involved in Sadaqa e Jariya on your behalf, praise be to Allah Whenever she helps a needy person and he/she prays for her in return, she tells them *"This is not from me, it is from Adam Ayub to you"*. Therefore Adam, even complete strangers pray for you. You are doing all this with the blessing of your Creator and the help of *Taray Janay Kay Baad*, praise be to Allah

I am grateful to you Adam, that Allah (SWT) put me on this path because of you. You are a means for me to do good in this world. Otherwise most parents get misled by Satan for the love of their children and thus fall prey to Satan's deceptions and also their ego. Such people lose their chances of success in the hereafter.

I heartily pray to Allah (SWT) to keep my intentions pure and sincere. May He accept all good deeds whether small or big. May He make all these deeds a source of permanent reward for you and us, Ameen.

Lots of prayers my child, Allah Hafiz.

Your Mother,
Urfana Ayub

Letter No 33.

Our tongues

My very dear son Adam Ayub,
Peace be upon you.
Lots of love and prayers.

How is my child today? Everyone here is fine. Time is passing. Seasons are changing. Daily the sun, moon, and stars rise and set. The weather of my heart and the weather of the world are in a process of constant change, but, my dear child, your memories are forever preserved in my heart. Today someone asked me, *"How many children do you have?"* I replied, *"Masha' Allah four"*. I count you in, even today. How can I possibly not remember you? You made me a mother for the very first time.

He is a memory, how can I erase it
He is my heartache how can I forget him
May you reach high levels I pray
May you exalt and reach the sky
May Allah (SWT) be your guardian forever
May high places of Heaven be yours (Ameen)

(Urfana Ayub)

Adam, I was trying to figure out - what is the one thing that elevates man, yet on the other hand causes him to fall in esteem? Do you know what that is? His own tongue. Our beloved prophet (PBUH) said about this piece of muscle:

"When man gets up in the morning, all the organs of the body acquire obedience before the tongue and say 'Be fearful of Allah in matters pertaining to us because we are connected with

164

you. If you keep right, we will also keep right. But if you falter (say wrong) we will also falter' (do wrong)"

Mishkah, Tirmidhi.

Usually we give full liberty to the tongue to utter whatever it feels like saying. There is no inhibition on it, neither is there any censorship for it. Before or during our speech, we do not think whether our words will embellish our hereafter or destroy it. This is because our worries are centred around this world only. Abdullah Ibn-e-Umer quotes our last Prophet (PBUH):

"He who keeps silent will succeed in the hereafter"

Tirmidhi

Our behavioural traits make us sin through our tongues. There is a long list of these behavioural sicknesses. To name just some: suspicion, inquisitiveness, *Gheebat* (backbiting), lies, criticising others, *La'anat* (cursing), Buhtan (accusing others of wrong which they have not done), anger, jealousy, constantly reminding others of the good you have done for them, *Keena* (malice), vulgar talk, making fun of others, mimicking others and regarding anyone as inferior to oneself in any respect.

Though these illnesses will not prove to be fatal in this life, but unfortunately, they will be a cause of eternal suffering in the hereafter. Interestingly, we do not consider such behaviour as a sickness in this life. According to most people, the diseases of this world are diabetes, high blood pressure, heart attack etc. We consult doctors for these diseases and take medicines for them, but we never think of treating illnesses of the tongue. There is only one foolproof therapy for these behavioral traits – exercising caution in your thoughts, refraining from saying or thinking bad things and safeguarding your tongue.

Whoever has control over his tongue will be saved from sin. Whoever guards himself against behavioural maladies will be saved from sin. He who fears Allah (SWT) will be saved from sin.

Adam, I think the most difficult task where man is highly tested is in his dealings with close relatives; how he uses his tongue with his family. We are always watching our words with outsiders; not so with our near and dear ones. Another point to understand is that each one of our relatives and the people around us deserves respect, because we are all dependent on one another. Every person on earth, no matter how beautiful, rich, talented or successful he may be, has to live his life with other people.

As a poet said:

Though it is bitter, still for the sake of shade
People plant Neem (bitter tree) in their garden

It is good that we pray for our benefit, but I am afraid that the sins of our tongue may rob us of our good deeds and impoverish us in the hereafter. As Abu Huraira quotes our beloved Prophet (PBUH):

"Do you know who is destitute"? His Sahaba replied "We think destitute is the person who does not have worldly riches". The

166

Prophet *(PBUH)* said: *"My Ummah's destitute is that person who will bring loads of Salah, Rozas (fast) and Zakat (charity) on the day of resurrection. During his/her life that person would have abused people, blamed them unjustly, usurped their money, wounded or killed people. All the oppressed will be given that person's good deeds. If his good deeds are exhausted before paying their debts, then those people's sins will be put in his account and he will be thrown in hell".*

Muslim

It is my prayer to Allah (SWT) Adam, that may He give us all, including myself, the ability to take care with our tongues. Let not our talk be a cause of pain to anyone and may everyone be protected from our tongues, Ameen.

I'm not afraid of thorns, but I dread the flowers
I dread those comments which injure my heart
I do not support ego, everyone is endeared
Those who bear ill will in heart, I dread those friends
I do not, in fact, like to sleep
For it shows false dreams and I dread these dreams
I care for all, I try to help others
Those who have a malice in their heart for me, I dread those relations
I belong to Allah (SWT) and I fear Him alone
Those who have no fear of Allah (SWT) I dread those people

(Unknown)

Adam I give you in Allah's (SWT) protection.

Your Mother

Inner peace

My dear child Adam Ayub,
Peace be upon you.
Lots of love and prayers.

My dear child, my heart has been feeling down since yesterday. It was your brother Arslan's birthday. Masha'Allah he turned 21. When I hugged him, tears started flowing from my eyes. For a long time I stood hugging him crying at the same time. The tears which were flowing were in your memory and also for Arslan's happiness.

You also turned 21 years of age after your departure. Adam, it is a coincidence that the date of your departure and that of Arslan's birthday are the same; the 27th. This date brings both grief and joy for me at the same time.

Adam, time is passing with the speed of light. Masha'Allah you are growing in the world of my heart. With changing times and situations your mother has become aware of the truths and intricacies of this finite life.

Adam, do you remember how much you loved football? Masha Allah, now your Dad, Chachcha's, brothers and cousins play football every week on a Saturday evening. Your Dad feels your absence very much. Adam, you spread so much love around you that people still remember and speak of you with affection. It is true that love begets love. If you spread hatred around, you will get hatred in return. If we want to get love, then we will have to take the first step to spread it. Praise be to Allah even today people praise your polite manners.

Abu Huraira quotes that our beloved Prophet (PBUH) was asked,

"Which action of people will cause most of them to enter Heaven?" He replied, "Abstinence from sins and good behaviour"

Tirmidhi

I pray to my Sustainer to award high ranks to my son in Heaven and grant him abode in *Jannat-ul-Firdous*, Ameen.

Good behaviour is a very valuable blessing of Allah (SWT). There are many people who live with every comfort in their life at their disposal, but they lack good behaviour. They do not realise how other people have to suffer and face problems because of their rude manner. It is also true that people who suffer at the hands of other people will finally find solace and comfort, because there is always light at the end of the tunnel. On the other hand, those who cause pain to others will keep wandering in search of peace.
As a poet said:

*Be warned when the world becomes your friend
For it takes very little time for it to change
Forget the things which you dream about
For it takes very little time to disrupt the sleep
Think before causing grief to anyone
For it takes very little time for their ill will to touch you
Lucky are those who receive love in life*

169

For it takes very little time for people to change tracks

Adam, I have learnt that inner peace only comes from remembering Allah. People may look for many other ways, but the hearts find peace only after remembrance and *Zikr* of Allah. If we do not find peace even after Allah's *Zikr*, we need to scrutinise our conduct. Have we been unjust to people? Are we earning money fairly? Our beloved Prophet (PBUH) said:

"Allah says find time for my Zikr, I will grant expanse in your endeavours; otherwise I will cause excess of worldly chores to press upon you so that you do not find free time and you will be devoid of peace"

Bukhari

Peace of mind is one of the biggest achievements of life. It is Allah's (SWT) pleasure and blessing. We cannot get peace in exchange for all our worldly possessions. The peace of heart is priceless. We cannot buy sleep. People take medicines to fall asleep, but even medicines cannot ensure a peaceful sleep.

Our dealings with Allah are all exchange programs. As long as we remember Allah, He also remembers us. The key to peace of mind is hidden in *Zikr* and thankfulness to Allah. The more grateful we are for Allah's bounties, the more He will bless us. It is Allah's promise to His people:

"If you thank me, I will grant you more"

Surah Ibrahim (Abraham), 14:7

Ungratefulness is an illness, which makes us restless and

170

narrow-minded. It destroys peace of mind. Whether we deal with Allah (SWT) or His people, we will remain restless until and unless we are thankful to both. An ungrateful person will inculcate this sickness in people around him. So we need to be extra wary of these ungrateful and thankless people.

Adam, we cannot become grateful creatures without knowledge of our religion. Islam teaches us qualities of patience, courage, wisdom, thankfulness and acceptance of one's fate. We cannot hope to attain gratitude without completely entering into the circle of Islam. Allah is well aware of our intentions. Islam is not like a bottle of water which we sip occasionally when we want to. Rather it is like blood which circulates in our body at all times.

Adam, while talking to you, I keep wandering from here and there. You are that companion of mine whose proximity I feel at all times and whom I love talking to.

May you be in Allah's protection my child.

Your Mother
Urfana Ayub

My desire versus your desire

Dear son Adam Ayub.
Peace be upon you.
Lots of love and prayers.

I missed you very much yesterday, my child. Do you know why? Yesterday your sister passed her driving test, but then what is the connection between her passing the test and me missing you? The strange thing is, Adam, that since you went away, I miss you and feel your absence very acutely on all happy and sad occasions. I get restless and cry my heart out. Then I feel peaceful. There are so many powerful emotions that I cannot name. These emotions are as strong and invincible as rocks, or like flowing water which can take you away from your destination so very quietly that you do not even realise. Yesterday I cried so much that I was forced to think about how strong and solid the ties of blood and the sentiments of motherhood can be.

Whenever I hear any good news, I want to share it with you, Adam. Your only sister is an adult now and driving. Ahmad is preparing for his GCSE examinations and Arslan is in the last year of university. All the children have grown up Masha'Allah.

Adam, when we hear of success in worldly exams, we are so happy that tears start flowing involuntarily. I wonder how we will feel when we get our final result in the hereafter. If we pass with good grades, we will be over the moon with joy Insha'Allah. I pray that may we all succeed in that exam and enter Jannat-ul-Firdous, Ameen.

We stretch ourselves to the limit chasing after these worldly exams. It is human nature to worry and plan for our future. There is hardly anybody who is not concerned about his future. But some people worry so much that they waste their present in the process. They forget that the present is in their hands. There is no logic or wisdom in losing our present in worries for tomorrow, but man spends all his life in this ignorance. Then, when the future does arrive, he yearns for the past and cries for it. If we think about it, Adam, a man does not benefit from past, present or future. During each, he keeps remembering and pining for another era and spends his life clinging to the memories, apprehensions and desires of those times.

Moreover, a person lives with so much vanity, insensitivity and callousness as if he will never die. During his time on earth, all his focus, endeavours and labours are directed towards attaining the deceptive goals of this life. He never thinks of death and so he does not make any preparations for it. He is not worried about the reality that if he is called back suddenly then he must have some luggage ready, e.g. good deeds, prayers, fulfilment of Allah's (SWT) and Prophet's (PBUH) rights. Alas, when such a person dies, within a very short time people start feeling as if he never lived at all.

As a poet said:

> *This, in fact, was your destination*
> *You spent your whole life reaching it*
> *What did you get in this world?*
> *Your own people buried you in the end*

At times Adam, I also feel that you never lived in this life. Sometimes it becomes difficult to believe that you also resided with us in this house. People express similar sentiments about deceased ones, feeling that the time they spent with them seems like a dream, like something unreal. You were a part of this family for nineteen years, but only five years after your departure I feel as if you never lived.

I have learnt from your departure that something which was not meant to be mine could never have been mine. When Allah's (SWT) order and decision comes, then my things do not remain mine any longer if they were not in my destiny. A few days back I made a cup of tea and brought it upstairs to my room. I put it on the side table. When I picked up the cup to drink, it slipped and fell on the floor spilling all the tea on the carpet. I could not drink even a sip of the tea because it was not in my destiny.

Similarly Adam, your daddy brought vegetable seeds for me from Pakistan. He made the garden beds ready for sowing them. The seed packets were lying next to empty packets for the rubbish. By mistake I threw all the packets in the dustbin without checking them. That same day the garbage collecting trucks came and emptied all our bins. The seeds were lost in the rubbish. When Daddy asked me about the seeds, I realised that I was not destined to use them. Had they been in our dustbin I could have retrieved the packets, but they had already gone in the garbage truck.

Aren't these Allah's (SWT) decisions Adam? The seeds had travelled all the way from Pakistan by airplane. Daddy spent quite some time and labour tilling the soil for sowing them, but when the actual time came for planting, the seeds had gone beyond my reach. There are innumerable such examples around us which we need to understand and accept.

When such incidents happened before, I reacted very strongly. I used to blame others for the loss, telling them that it was due to their negligence. But since you went away Adam, I have learnt that if a particular thing is not in my destiny, I could never have it. Even if that thing comes to my house and remains a part of my life, it will go away since it was never mine. It is Allah's decision that He made something our destiny for a specific time, but then takes it away per his divine decree. This feeling makes me content with what I have received and also removes the fears, and suspicions of past, present and future.

It is obligatory for every Muslim to accept all of Allah's (SWT) decisions wholeheartedly and with full understanding. Allah's orders are clearly stated in the holy Qur'an. As Allah says in Qur'an:

"But as for him who turns away from my remembrance, he will have a suffocated life, and We will raise him up blind on the Day of Resurrection. He will say: 'O my Lord! why have You raised me up blind, while I possessed sight (before)?' [Allah (SWT)] will say: 'Thus did you, when Our signs came to you, you forgot them: so will you, this day, be forgotten'."

Surah Ta-Ha, 20:124-126

Here *"signs"* means Allah's commands as well as His creations, which are all in fact Allah's signs. These are Allah's (SWT) decisions which we must accept as our destiny without complaining about why something happened to us. We are

175

all Allah's (SWT) creations. He is our real owner. He decides whatever He wills regarding us and He has full authority and control.

May Allah grant us all the courage and ability to live our lives with open eyes and insight. May He resurrect us on the Day of Judgment with sight, Ameen.

There is a *Hadeeth-i-Qudsi* which means:

"Oh children of Adam there are things I want and there are things which you want. Things which I want are bound to happen. Thus if you entrust yourself to My will then I will grant you what you wish, but if you go against My will then I will despair you in your desires and ultimately My will shall prevail."

Allah Hafiz.

Your Mother,
Urfana Ayub

I miss you my Adam

Dear Adam,

How are you my child? I have full faith in my Creator that He will make your grave one of the gardens of paradise Insha'Allah. You spread love among other people as long as you lived in this world. None of your relatives had any complaints about you. I remember that you never even quarrelled with your siblings when you were young. You never dirtied your clothes either.

Young children are very naughty. Their clothes need changing many times during the day, but you were never like that. When you started school, your uniform used to be so clean that I wondered whether to wash it or not. You were always fine in your habits and behaviour. Nobody ever complained that *"Adam picked a fight with somebody or beat someone"*. You grew up without causing trouble. You used to greet everyone with respect. You were a favourite with everybody and my very dear friend.

Adam, you were always very patient. Even though you went through many ups and downs in your health, you faced them with patience and courage. I don't know how much you suffered. I will never forget that time when, while on your deathbed, you asked why Daddy and I had tears in our eyes. Those moments are lodged in my mind. You looked at us with love in your eyes and asked in your feeble voice, *"Mum why are you crying?"* Then you wiped my tears with your hands. When Daddy took my place and sat next to you, you repeated your question. *"Daddy, why are you crying?"*

Then you wiped Daddy's tears with your fingers. Do you know, Adam, why we were crying then? Because doctors had told us to have a family time, because you would leave this world very soon.

I still have not understood the truth about life. Is it that fragile, just like a delicate thread? Is time so powerful? Is man so weak and helpless?

It is not that I have not accepted the fact, Nauzobillah, but these questions keep reminding me of the truth about life.

The lesson was not even written in any book
Which I learnt from time and life experiences

Your departure also revealed to me that the studies of this world, its degrees and different courses are unable to teach us the truth about life and the world.

The lesson which Allah (SWT) taught me, which I witnessed with my own eyes, was your departure from this world. I had never studied this lesson in any book, Adam! The experiences of this world make man wise. They teach us lessons full of wisdom which cannot be found in any school or college book.

Sometimes Adam, I miss you very intensely like today. My tears need no permission to flow, neither are they limited by place, time or location. They are masters of their own will. Tears are also one of Allah's (SWT) blessings. We feel light after shedding tears. Whenever I read this couplet, I instinctively think of you!

That one face which had found abode in my eyes
Remained confined in my tears the whole life

Adam, when my thoughts turn to you, I cannot confine your memories. It is beyond my control, just like dried up leaves which keep moving in the wind. No matter how much I chase after them, I cannot gather these leaves.

As a poet describes:

While looking for you on the roads of memory
I disperse like dried leaves daily

Adam, never ever think that I am not happy. However, whenever I remember you I become very sad. You are a part of my being. It was because of you I became a mother for the first time. I taught your small feet how to walk. By the grace of Allah (SWT) I taught you how to speak. I polished you by good training and correct manners. I cannot forget that 19-year journey in just five years. People often say that memories fade with time. But I feel that you will "live" here more than any of us, even after leaving this world.

Praise be to Allah you actively participate in all good deeds even today. May Allah elevate your ranks. May He make you a source of permanent reward for us all, may He give you a high place in Jannat-ul-Firdous and may He make me meet my son, Ameen. I will wait for our meeting my child, Insha'Allah.

As a poet said:

Though he left me a long time back

He did not go away from my sight for even a while

Your memory, the experience of you in my life, did not leave me for even a moment. But Adam, when I think of it, five years seems a very long period. Sometimes the thought strikes me - did you ever even came to this world or not?

With lots of prayers and good wishes I entrust you to the protection of my Lord.

Your Mother,
Urfana Ayub

Letter No 37.

Cruel behaviour

Dear son Adam Ayub,

When I hear of instances of injustice and brutality, I am forced to ask what types of hearts these people possess? What kind of people can sleep peacefully after doing injustice to others? Are their hearts made up of some other material? Or are they of a different shape?

Then my mind answers that Allah (SWT) made man the most superior of all His creations. Everyone possesses the same heart which is a type of muscle. Then why do we have such different attitudes? How can some people amongst us treat others with inhuman brutality?

Adam I heard of a true but bitter story today. A few young bullies punished a poor lad who was selling eggs because he asked for payment when he sold the eggs to those spoilt boys. They hung him upside down from a tree. That child kept hanging the whole night and died in the morning. The savage youths killed an innocent lad for a few rupees; money which that boy had earned and was his right, Allahu -Akbar. I boil with rage on hearing such incidents. I fail to understand how it is possible that, in an Islamic society, we so-called *"Muslims"* do not give others their rights and treat them so viciously.

The Holy Qur'an talks about injustice in several places:

1. *"Allah (SWT) does not guide the wrongdoing people."*

    Surah Ale-Imran (The Family of Imran), 3:86

2. *"Unquestionably, the curse of Allah (SWT) is upon the wrong doers."*

    Surah Hood (Prophet Hud), 11:18

3. *Allah (SWT) does not love the wrongdoers."*

    Surah Ale-Imran (The Family of Imran), 3:57

4. *"The unjust shall have no compassionate friend nor any intercessor who would be listened to."*

    Surah Ghafir (The Forgiver or The Believer), 40:18

All these Ayat prove that the unjust and wrongdoers will gain Allah's (SWT) curse, not His love. Such people will find no friend or helper and their hearts will become rigid from being distant from Allah's (SWT) blessings.

As a poet said:

> *Be kind to the creatures on the earth*
> *Allah (SWT) will be kind to you in the skies*

It is said that if you learn to live with humility on this earth, then you will find peace beneath it as well. Islam teaches us to be kind, compassionate and forgiving. Allah (SWT) likes kindness. He is all-forgiving and compassionate.

Mother's womb is called Raham (kindness) because a baby develops within it. Allah (SWT) nurtures a beautiful live child inside the darkness of mother's womb. When the same child grows up, he becomes a creature of injustice and savagery. Adam, we are not born like this! Every child is born innocent like a clean slate and his nature is as defined by our religion, which is soft-hearted and just. This child is trained by his parents and society. That is why our religion lays so much emphasis on good training of children. It is easy to bear children, but very difficult to raise them according to the principles of Islam which should be the goal of every parent. In general we cater for the physical needs of our children, like food, clothes etc., but we ignore or forget to provide for their spiritual wellbeing, which is to connect our children with Allah (SWT). We must explain to them the reason and objective of their creation. Yet all our endeavours are focused on making our child a success in society with a good job, a beautiful house and a big car.

I don't know which world we are living in! We have to meet Allah (SWT) one day and account for all that we did and said in this world. Is my luggage ready for that big day? Have I made preparations for the final journey? Is my suitcase ready in which I need lots of good deeds rather than clothes and other material things?

Is my handbag all packed which I must fill with pure deeds performed according to Allah's (SWT) commands and the Prophet's (PBUH) way of life, rather than worldly things? Do I have enough goodies to fill my bag? Or will I embark on my final journey with an empty handbag and suitcase? I know that if we plan to travel somewhere, even for a few days, we take luggage with us because *"it is not right to go empty-handed"*. Now just imagine the place where we will spend our entire life; an eternal, never-ending life. We need a lot of luggage to take along, otherwise extreme embarrassment and shame will be our destiny because our ignorance and idleness made us go forth with empty hands.

Adam, I feel our relationship with Allah (SWT) is like that of a tenant. Allah (SWT) is our landlord. He has rented this world to us to reside in, but the terms of agreement state that we must live in accordance with Allah's (SWT) commands and the way of life of our Prophet (PBUH). But what are we doing? We have tried to become the landlord instead of tenant. We are going totally against the terms of the contract. We are unfair with people and neither do we give our creator His due right and respect. This is injustice!

Injustice means not giving rights to the ones who are entitled to the same. When children do not give rights to their parents, they are unjust to the parents. When we do not fulfil Allah's (SWT) orders, and do not show Him the obedience which is expected of us, we are unjust towards Allah (SWT). Our Creator is very generous and lenient towards us, but we must dread the time when Allah's (SWT) wrath befalls us. We must never forget that, though He has given us leeway and leverage in this world, we have to face Him in the hereafter one day.

It is our Creator's extreme benevolence and magnanimity that, despite our disobedience, He has not evicted us from our house. On the contrary, any landlord of this world would turn us out in no time if we break the terms of the contract.

I was talking to a lady who told me that her mother-in-law took her to Umrah when she had recently given birth to her baby. She was not even in a state of cleanliness for the holy journey. Thus she could not engage herself in *Ibadah* (prayer), nor did she have the physical strength to perform the ritual. She was elated of course to be going on Umrah, but her mother-in-law's objective in taking her along was only to be an attendant. The poor woman left her newborn baby with her in-laws and accompanied her mother-in-law as a helper. Due to her ill health and physical weakness, the young mother could not perform Umrah and spent the entire time as a servant, doing chores for her mother-in-law.

Do not give us that power O Lord
That we do not see anything besides our own selves

(Bashir Badar)

Adam it is not necessary that a helpless and oppressed person has to voice his grief.

As a poet said:

Those familiar with art of writing can read
The story of grief is written on faces

We are the followers of that blessed Prophet (PBUH) who was so considerate towards the mothers of infants that he shortened the prayer for them.

Respected Anas Bin Malik (RA) said,

"I have never offered more comprehensive yet considerate

185

Salah behind anyone except our beloved Prophet (PBUH). If during prayer he heard a child crying he would shorten the prayer lest the child's mother would get upset"

Bukhari

Adam I do not understand how anyone could be so cruel and show so much selfishness for their near and dear ones that he/she would be unjust towards family even whilst sitting in Allah's (SWT) house. I was shaken to the core when I heard that young mother's story and I felt like crying. Is our heart made of flesh or stone?

Why do we pardon all the mistakes and sins of our own children and penalise others' for crimes they did not commit? Our own son is in the right, even when he is not able to fulfil the duties of a husband and the daughter-in-law is accused of being sterile even when she is completely healthy! O Lord, please let our hearts be pieces of flesh in which You and Your fear reside. Please make us all, including myself, follow the right path. The path where we are able to see our mistakes and which makes our hearts soft, Ameen.

رَبَّنَا لَا تُزِغْ قُلُوبَنَا بَعْدَ إِذْ هَدَيْتَنَا وَهَبْ لَنَا

مِن لَّدُنكَ رَحْمَةً ۚ إِنَّكَ أَنتَ الْوَهَّابُ *

"Our Lord! Let not our hearts deviate now after You have guided us and grant us mercy from Your own presence. Indeed You are the bestower of bounties without measure."

Surah Ale-Imran (The Family of Imran), 3:8

My child, my heart has become very depressed by sharing all this. O Allah (SWT) grant satisfaction to our hearts, Ameen.

Dear Lord, I entrust my child to you.

Your Humble Servant,
Urfana Ayub

Mending relations

My dear son Adam Ayub,
Peace be upon you.
My sincerest prayers and lots of love for you.

Adam, do you know what hurts me most? When people misunderstands me. Maybe it is human nature that people can take what you are saying the wrong way despite dealing with them in all sincerity. Then it really hurts.

I think every one of us experiences such an occurrence at times in our lives. Situations get worse due to misunderstandings, or sometimes we simply fail to recognise another's sincerity.

People's cold attitudes, criticism and bitter comments are more injurious than a sharp knife. If you also treated people as badly as they have treated you, then perhaps you might not feel so wounded when others take offense with your comments or behaviour, but if your dealings are based on truth and sincerity and still others do not believe, acknowledge and respect that, then hearts are shattered into thousands of fragments. Yet nobody outside even hears a sound or comes to know about it. The affected person ends up injuring himself trying to pick up the pieces. Sometimes we keep tolerating these insults for a while and finally we become quiet, because we feel that no amount of explanation or talking will help.
As a poet said:

> *The lull of the ocean says to the river's turbulence*
> *The more dignity a man has the more quiet he is*

At times people even start questioning your silence and mistake it for something else.

Adam, I have learnt two important things from my life. You never have to give explanations to people who truly know you, because such people would never doubt your intentions. On the other hand a person who does not know you will never be satisfied even if you offer a thousand explanations for your actions.

The second important thing - a person's open mindedness is reflected in his/her talk and character. It requires an open mind to praise others. I do not mean that you start writing poetry praising others for everything they do, but a little appreciation is necessary at times for encouragement. I have observed a definite stinginess in most people regarding praise.

Every person has his own opinion regarding praise. Sometimes praise makes the other person proud and boastful. I agree that at times compliments can go to one's head, which is why the intention of the person complementing and the attitude of the one being praised are equally important. We praise our children so that they get encouragement and are motivated, but we cannot compliment someone else's child because our ego does not allow us to do so. Like, "My daughter is one in a million". The entire world's praise is directed towards her because she happens to be "my" daughter. But a daughter-in-law with similar or better qualities will not earn a single word of praise from her mother-in-law because it requires a lot of courage and substance to praise others.

Our beloved Prophet (PBUH) said:

"If a person receives something and he has the ability to pay for it then he should pay the other person. If he cannot repay then he must praise the other person. He who praises offers thanks and he who hides it, is thankless".

Abi Daud, Kitab ul Adab (The book of general behaviour): 483

Sometimes people, in particular family members, will continue making sacrifices in the hope of befriending someone so that they will finally be acknowledged. In return some people can overcome their vanity and praise another person genuinely. But as a general rule, one human being cannot respect another human being. He/she simply wants to get all the respect himself/herself and be put on a high pedestal of honour and dignity for everyone to see. Yet this same individual is not prepared to give status or due rights to anyone else. Such selfish behaviour often indicates a lack of substance in a person.

Prestige cannot be weighed in the balance of boasts
Character cannot be measured by a measuring tape

(Muzaffar Warsi)

Adam, I pray to Allah (SWT) not to let me offend anyone. I apologise to everyone whose heart I have broken knowingly or unintentionally. O Allah (SWT) let not anyone be offended by me. Make me a righteous person who collects others' good wishes and prayers, Ameen.

O my Lord give me enough insight to recognise the sincere love of my relatives. Let me acknowledge and be thankful to them.

You know Adam, I have always kept my extended family in very high esteem. I have acknowledged and respected them praise be to Allah (swt). I was never a person who wanted money, houses or other worldly benefits. Wherever there was even the slightest chance of straining relationships, I simply abandoned that path and tried my level best to compromise.

If we have all the wealth of the world, but do not have family, we are poor. We are destitute despite having money. Some people have no riches, but they enjoy peace of mind and have love and respect for each other. These people are rich despite having no material things. Adam, I also want to be such a rich person. Let me be a person who forges relationships and not the one who breaks them.

As Muslims we are all well aware of the importance of *Silah e Rahmi* (family ties). Adam, at times trying to maintain relationships within the extended family becomes life's toughest test because some people are very difficult to appease. No matter how softly you try to deal with them, they make things difficult. Some people are victims of suspicion and thinking ill of others. Again, no matter how sincerely and sympathetically you treat such people, their suspicions poison the entire relationship. Suspicion is that illness, which, in my knowledge, has no cure except trust in Allah (SWT).

Sayyadna Abu Huraira narrates,

"A man came to our beloved Prophet (PBUH) and said 'There

are some relatives of mine with whom I try to maintain relations but they break ties with me. I try to be good to them but they behave badly towards me. I deal with patience and endurance but they act stupidly'. The Prophet (PBUH) replied, 'If you act as you are telling me then it is as though you are putting hot ashes into their mouths and there will be a helper from Allah (SWT) who would always stand by you against them as long as your behaviour remains the same'."

Muslim, Kitab ul Tuhf

Yet despite understanding the importance of *Silah e Rahmi*, sometimes relatives and circumstances bring you to such a painful place that keeping a distance is the only solution to ensure peace.

As a poet said:

By going places
By increasing connections
The love fades out
And leads to slander
So I've concluded
It is best to stay distant

If at any time we want to discover the amount of goodness we possess, we must all assess our capacity to pardon others just for the sake of Allah (SWT). Develop the habit and the courage to pardon others. It is Allah's (SWT) special blessing that He Has concealed the sins of man, because if we were shown each other's wrongdoings, we would not even bury one another.

Hadhrat Ali (RA) says,

"The real beauty of life is not how happy you are, rather the actual beauty of life is how happy you have made others"

The key to gain entry into Heaven is hidden in the following Hadith of our beloved Prophet (PBUH). He was asked, *"How far is Heaven?"* The Prophet (PBUH) replied, *"Heaven is just a journey of two steps. Put your first step on your desires and your second step will be in Heaven."*

We must never forget that in this world everyone owns varying assets - houses, cars and other material things - but everyone's grave will be the same size.

May Allah (SWT) make our hearts so large and exalt our consciences to such an extent that we stand by truth always, and when dealing with our relatives, we must correct our shortcomings and avoid the injustice of undermining other people's sincerity, Ameen.

Your Mother,
Urfana Ayub

Letter No 39.

Physical and Spiritual development

Lots of love and loads of prayers for my dearest Adam Ayub. Who bade farewell to the love of dear ones and inhabited the silence of the grave!

Adam, I often wonder how weak and naive man is! He builds lots of protective walls around him, yet within all these physical shields he is just a spirit *(Rooh)* covered in flesh. No matter how strong or hard a man seems to be from the outside, he can feel the pain of a pinprick just like anyone else. He also feels happy when respected, just like other people. The difference lies in the way we express our attitudes.

Some people are over the moon when happy and others become proud and think of themselves as far superior to others. The point is - both are happy but the expression of happiness is different.

Both types of person will eat when they are hungry. Though what they eat is different, it will still be food which fills their stomachs. Similarly, when thirsty, everyone whether king or beggar, drinks water. No other liquid in this world can quench the thirst as water does.

What do we require? Our basic necessities are food, clothes and a home/shelter. The wish to be wanted, loved and respected is shared by all in every station of life.

Everyone feels bad and belittled when insulted unjustly. A

poor man may not dare to react and stays silent instead, but an influential person could show a violent reaction. One must understand that both are equally hurt.

When someone is wounded due to another person's bad temper, he needs healing for his injuries. The remedies consist of love, sympathy, respect, empathy, trust and understanding.

Some people's attitudes are so insulting that they batter the very spirit of others by their poisonous words. These people may not realise that they have abused the other person's love to such an extent that the injured party will fall ill unless some treatment is administered.

As a poet said:

*You do not even know that someone has shattered completely,
Whilst trying to strengthen the bonds of love*

We often need external creams and bandages. If a finger is cut while chopping vegetables or fruit, we immediately try to stop the bleeding by applying a plaster, but no one considers the invisible internal wounds.

We pay so much attention to external beauty and spend lots of money and time on it, but have we ever thought of our spiritual condition? We are ignorant of how much our spiritual health has deteriorated.

When we look in the mirror, we all scrutinise our faces for blemishes, spots, dryness, unwanted hair, etc, and we are willing to apply different creams and bleaches, or get facials, waxing and threading to enhance our beauty. At the shops we see rows of products from big brand names claiming to improve our looks. These include face masks and all sorts of creams, which are equally popular among men and women.

For just our hands and feet alone, many measures are employed to take care of them, such as manicures, pedicures, lotions, massage and creams, to name just a few.

Take the hair! The variety of shampoos, conditioners, hair oils, gels, creams, sprays and other products which can be used is immense.

Both men and women are equally concerned about hair colour and hairstyle. Since good healthy hair enhances our looks, a lot of the time, money and attention is spent on it. Baldness is the focus of attention of many men. Sometimes they try conventional therapies, or they may resort to expensive and painful procedures like hair transplants. Wigs are commonly used.

A substantial percentage of men and women spend a lot of money on clothes. They wear attractive, trendy styles to look beautiful. They take care to match their outfits with their personalities. They splash out on designer wear from famous boutiques to stay a step ahead so that by wearing these labels they can proudly boast about their fashion sense. Even toddlers now wear designer outfits. People buy designer dresses and shoes even for their newborns.

Adam, I do not mean that everyone has adopted this lifestyle, but it is spreading fast.

Our spirit has thousands of creases
Though not a wrinkle is shown in the dress

(Shakaib Jalali)

People notice you from head to toe. Shoes are a major source of interest. What type and colour and which brand you are wearing?

We humans are so particular about everything from head to toe. We are obsessed with all the fine details of our clothes and shoes, but why isn't anybody concerned about their inner self? What is our interior world like? What season is it passing through?

A person takes a lot of care if his physical health deteriorates. He consults good doctors and specialists and takes medicines. If the illness affects his heart then he takes extra care and precautions. He will adopt a special diet and exercise programme to get better. The external ailments get cured, but no one is worried about our internal state and spiritual well-being.

There are thousands of diseases of the heart which erode it's very core. They cancel out all our good deeds, but we have turned a blind eye to them. We do not realise that they also require treatment.

After becoming connected with the Qur'an, I have understood that Qur'an is like a mirror for us. Not only does it show our external form and figure, but it also reveals the depths of our souls. The light of the Qur'an's teachings removes the dark sheet of ignorance from our shortcomings.

Adam, I am ever thankful to my Creator for granting me the ability to understand Qur'an. I fervently pray that my actions and deeds also change accordingly in a positive manner. I also pray that, before I point out other people's mistakes, let me analyse myself. May Allah (SWT) make me aware of my mistakes so that I can rectify them before my death, Ameen. Let me live my life according to the principle: *"Look for evil in your own self and goodness in others"* Ameen.

When I concentrated, I discovered many illnesses in my inner being. I found myself to be like a broken and worn out building, the walls of which were in a precarious condition. Somewhere a window was broken and in other places the paint was coming off. The doors were in need of repair and in spots the foundation was found wanting.

Praise be to Allah , Qur'an made me realise that a lot of work needs to be done. Widespread repairs are necessary. When one's own building requires so much repair work, how can we point out mistakes in other's buildings?

I pray that may Allah (SWT) help me strengthen the foundation of my spiritual being. Let me plaster the walls of my building, let me put the paint of resolution where required. And O Lord, give me the ability to change all the doors and windows which have been installed by the absurd norms of our society before I finally return to You.

I could see others' errors while I was ignorant of myself
When I saw my own shortcomings, no one else seemed at fault

(Bahadur Shah Zafar)

At times we worship people. We respect them and put them on a high pedestal that they do not deserve. This is usually done out of blind love, or due to their relationship to us or position. But when we get a chance to get to know them, they turn out to be opposite of what we had thought. Sometimes they even hurt us, but one thing is certain. These people disguise their failings so brilliantly that you get deceived time and again.

Don't they say that sugar and salt resemble each other? Both are the same colour, but the difference becomes apparent when we taste them. The same applies to people.

I pray to Allah (SWT) to let my exterior be as my inner self and change my inner self to match what I appear to be on the outside.

If there is any hypocrisy or conflict between my speech and actions, please remove them. If I do not like a particular thing for myself, then I should not like it for my brother or sister either. There is a Hadeeth of our Prophet (PBUH),

"None amongst you will be complete in Imaan unless he loves for his brother what he loves for himself."

Bukhari Kitab-ul-Iman (The book of faith) 13

Adam, you may be wondering what type of discussion your mother has started. Sometimes I do not even realise what I keep writing. When I want to talk to you and share my views with you, I start writing.

Sometimes I discuss one point and then switch to another.

The truth is, my imagination wanders on untrodden paths when you are my companion. I like your company, my child. I fully understand that you cannot hear me, nor will you read my letters, but it's very satisfying to know that I can share my thoughts with you. It is just as someone walking barefoot on hot sand in a desert would feel comforted when he walks on soft and fresh grass.

Adam, I do not think my writing style is very impressive, but people encouraged me a lot after *Taray Janay Kay Baad* and motivated me to keep writing. Thank you Adam, for teaching me and encouraging me to write. All the passions which I had nurtured since my childhood have been fulfilled, but never in my dreams did I ever think of writing. It is said *"necessity is the mother of invention"* and true to this phrase, your memory taught me to write.

I feel that my writing should be of benefit to people. Otherwise the whole purpose of writing is defeated. *Taray Janay Kay Baad* gave me comfort, peace and personal satisfaction. Masha'Allah people have benefited from it a lot. I have started writing again after a gap of five years, and I pray that may Allah (SWT) bless it and make it a source of permanent reward for you, me and all those who buy or read it, Ameen.

May you be in Allah's (SWT) protection, my child.

Your Mother,
Urfana Ayub

Karachi, my city

My dear son and friend Adam Ayub,
Thousands of sincere prayers and lots of love.

Adam, these days news from Pakistan disturbs me badly. It seems as though our country is under someone's curse or else we are disobeying Allah's (SWT) orders and the present situation is a punishment for that. Allah (SWT) says in the holy Qur'an:

> *"And whatever strikes you of disaster - it is for what your hands have earned; but He pardons much"*

Surah Ash-Shurah (The Consultation), 42:30

I grieve over the situation of the entire country, but my town Karachi has become the centre of news. Every other news headline is about Karachi. The whole city is rampaged by restlessness and chaos. People do not feel safe going out of their houses because everyone fears for their lives. People go out only for essential errands.

Adam, I cherish my beautiful childhood memories of Karachi. When I was young, Karachi was referred to as *"The City of Lights"*. It was a peaceful city then. We could go to market whenever we wanted to. The whole city used to be alive till late at night. The seaside area of Clifton used to be crowded with people. Inhabitants of other cities and villages came to Karachi in search of jobs. It was considered to be a successful city of business and trade. There was so much peace that people slept outside on the footpaths without any fears.

As time passed, the situation changed and Karachi became a city of terror. Now people dread going out of their houses. Nobody goes to Karachi for recreation or tourism. Markets close early. Shops are often closed due to strikes. Now no one sleeps on the footpaths. Darkness prevails over the entire city. Many people have moved their businesses and jobs to other cities or countries. Daily the news bulletins are packed with items about Karachi, like a bomb blast or shooting in a Masjid (mosque) or a public place - how many innocent children were killed, how many thefts and robberies took place etc.

Adam, my heart bleeds at all this. One's homeland, city, the soil of the country; all these are beautiful links. No matter where a person goes, he will always remain connected to the place where he was born and spent the beautiful carefree days of childhood.

I long for my city. Whenever I go to Pakistan, I try to visit my school and college buildings and show my children the place where I was educated.

Adam, that time was so wonderful. We used to play outdoors with other children without any fear. We used to ride on bikes. Nowadays people are afraid to let their children leave the house. Adam, I also feel pity for the children who are confined indoors in an artificial world of smartphones, TV and games. They do not get a chance to meet and interact with other children.

Adam, I often think of this poem about my city Karachi.

The city of Karachi never slept
Darkness never prevailed over houses
Sounds of buses disturbed the sleep
As though night never fell on these
The roasting of peanuts on carts
The streets used to be awake till night
Its people loved each other
Which was like a thorn in the heart of the enemies
Then there was a conspiracy
With lots of killings in the vicinity
There was devastation in Karachi
And deaths in many houses
Now everything is dark
If we survive we will see the morning's spark

Adam, peace is what is needed by the whole world, not only Karachi. This discord is eroding every nook and cranny of our country like a termite and we need a dose of peace to get rid of it. Peace and love are the foremost desires of the people of every country, city, town and village. We want to live our lives with harmony and accord in such a serene environment that our hearts sing with joy when we wake up in the morning, and when night falls we can go to our houses free from fear.

In every country and town, people of all colours and tribes have one craving and desire and that is peace.

Islam conveys the best possible message of peace and harmony. Followers are ordained not only to be good to fellow Muslims, but to deal amicably and sociably with the non-Muslim as well. Our beloved Prophet (PBUH) has also taught us that no Arab is superior to a non-Arab and a white man has no advantage over a black man. Only the person who is more Allah-fearing (Taqwa) has an advantage over others. But today the Shia Muslims and Sunni Muslims are killing each other. One sect of Muslims is thirsty for the blood of the other sect.

Adam, the whole world is suffering from killings and massacres. When will peace prevail here? These evil disasters are increasing day by day.

Adam, I remember with longing the Dua which we used to recite in our school assembly in which we pray to Allah (SWT):

My heartiest desire comes to my lips in the form of a prayer
Oh Lord let my life be like a flare
Let my country be adorned by me
Just like a garden is adorned by its flowers
Let my life be like a light bug
So that I may love the light of knowledge
Let me support the poor
And love the old and dire
Oh Lord protect me from every evil
Make me follow the path of right (Ameen)

(Allama Iqbal)

Your Mother,
Urfana Ayub

Destiny

My very dear son Adam Ayub,

How is my child? I came to visit you yesterday, Adam. You were peacefully asleep in your grave oblivious to the whole world. All our associations with this world last only while we live. The moment death takes over, concerns and worries for our next journey begin. We all have to pray for the journey into eternal life. In this selfish world where no one is sincere to the other, how can we expect anyone to pray for a mound of mud?

Life teaches a lot of things, but this learning is entirely different from what we get in school and colleges. The cruel book of life first makes you face many tough tests and then leaves the newly learnt lesson etched in your mind and heart which can never be erased from memories. In contrast, worldly education teaches lessons first and then gives the exams. Life's book is far more difficult and complicated than worldly books. It is indifferent to age and teaches lessons to young and old alike.

As a poet said:

How times keep changing
I'm not that old, but have learnt many lessons

During life, most of us are under the false impression that we are extremely attractive and wise. We are very proud of our children and wealth, but Adam, I have found myself to be completely powerless in the hands of destiny. Ammi used to recite this poem to me:

Wisdom says I'm superior
I know what's going on everywhere
Wealth says I am superior
The world follows me everywhere
Beauty says I am the prettiest
World feasts its eyes on me
You are all liars the destiny insists
I will make happen whatever I wish

Adam, destiny is always the winner. Wisdom, wealth and beauty cannot stand before destiny. Allah (SWT) grants these bounties to whoever He wishes and gives them in abundance to many, while many other people keep yearning and struggling for these things throughout life.
As a poet said:

Some people come and take it
Others crave their life for it
O Lord I have no complaints
Everyone comes with a different destiny

Belief in destiny only comes if one has true Imaan, patience and courage. One must understand that everyone gets according to his share, as this saying illustrates:

What is the difference between two walking feet?
One is in front the other behind
Neither the front foot is proud nor the hind foot meek
Because they know their positions will alter in no time
Exactly this is life!

Adam everything is finite. Yesterday, I went to a friend's place to console her on the death of her Taya (elder brother of her father). She told me that her Taya had been perfectly well. He spent the entire day according to his usual routine and offered his prayers. Her Tayi (Taya's wife) had gone to her daughter's house to spend the night, so there was no one at home with the Taya that evening. He went to the kitchen to prepare food for himself and died there of a heart attack. In the morning when he did not answer anyone's phone call, the family came looking for him and found his dead body on the kitchen floor.

Adam, now Muslims in the UK have the facility to opt for a scan instead of a post mortem, praise be to Allah (SWT). So when the Taya's body was scanned, it was discovered that he died the previous night.

Hearing about this death brought this expression to mind:

"The world is a service station not the destination"

When we embark on a long journey, we usually stop for a while at a service station to rest, refuel, attend to our needs, wash, and eat and drink. Motorway services are meant for these things only. If we try to buy land, build a house or search for a job there, tell me Adam, how will we get to our destination?

There are two ways to live your life in this world - as you desire or as your Creator desires.

The life of our choice is one where there are no limitations and it is completely under the control of our desires. On the contrary, in the life of Allah's (SWT) choice, one has to suppress one's ego and aim to please only Allah (SWT).

I pray that may we live the life of Allah's (SWT) choice so that we can reach our chosen destination. Let us take this world as a service station and not our destiny, Ameen. Whenever the candle of our desires is about to blow out in the strong winds of destiny, we must hold on to patience and be content with Allah's (SWT) decisions.

It is evil to shatter a broken heart
Allah is with those who don't have anyone else
I will not beg for happiness from you
Borrowed wealth is of use to no one
People for no reason call bad names for someone who has no control
People are good, it is time which is merciless
Why should I complain of my destruction?
Whatever is there in my destiny, I am bound to get it

(Munir Niazi)

I give you in Allah's (SWT) protection my child.

Your Mother,
Urfana Ayub

Children

To my dear son Adam Ayub,
who familiarised me with the eternal life hidden behind
death, which in turn is harboured by temporary life,
peace be upon you.

My heart is grieving today. It is because of my meeting
with a mother who is so fed up with her children's insolent
behaviour and rebellion that she has decided never to see
her children again in her life nor keep any connection with
them. Crying ceaselessly, the woman told me this was the
toughest decision of her life and she took it because she
was extremely hurt and helpless. Otherwise, which mother
would wish to be parted from her kids? She had brought
them up with patience and pain. Now her bitter words are
echoing in my ears.

*"When you do not have children you yearn for a child, but I wish
I was childless rather than having these insensitive children. At
least I would not have to face these times."*

Today I saw a mother's love being harmed by her own children.
Adam, Allah (SWT) blesses mothers with extreme patience
and courage and an amazing amount of softness for their
children, but when her patience is stretched to its limits by
children's insolent behaviour, when the naked ruthlessness
of kids breaks a mother's courage, and when her selfless love
and tenderness fails to evoke respect, then a mother's heart
is shattered. Something similar happened with this mother
today, Adam. I could do nothing for her except console her

and ask her to remain calm and patient.

May Allah (SWT) grant sabr (patience) to all those parents whose children's torture has caused them to age early. And may Allah (SWT) give guidance to those non-conscientious children before their loving and ever-praying parents leave this world and they do not get a chance to say sorry!

Our beloved Prophet (PBUH) said:

"Unlucky is the person who does not earn his parents' prayers by serving them and then keeps on asking others to pray for him"

Adam I am genuinely worried for those disobedient and rebellious children who do not respect relationships and tarnish their hereafter during this life. Mostly by the time they come to the right path or realise the parents' worth, it is too late. They then live lives of painful regret because their own conscience keeps pricking them.

Our feeling of shame at doing something wrong is Allah's (SWT) blessing in disguise. Keeping parents pleased and satisfied is the best way to earn Heaven. That person is unlucky who does not earn this blessing for himself even when both his parents are alive.

Good, pious children adorn this life and the hereafter for their parents. Otherwise, love for children can be such a test and trial that even affects one's fate. Adam, I have seen people disregarding relationships for the love of their children. People even ignore their parents for the benefit of their children. Blind love for children distances them from their brothers and sisters. People sacrifice their blood relatives for the sake of their children. Some parents shower unconditional and extreme love on their children and others mercilessly sever all other bonds for their sake.

A sacrifice is also a kind of test, which can only be made for love, especially for the love of those who are very dear to you. Parents give up their wealth, energy and time for their children. But in the process they could treat their other family members unjustly and thus destroy their Hereafter.

Adam, I feel that children are like a very sweet fruit whose sweetness is absorbed in the very being of parents and they cannot abandon it despite wanting to. Sometimes too much of this sweetness becomes a poison for parents. But it can also become a source of envy for those couples who are deprived of this blessing. Over-indulgent, boastful parents can keep reminding such couples of the emptiness in their lives.

Adam, the truth is that only Allah (SWT) knows which bounty to bless and to whom; like which of His people will be blessed with good health, a fine husband, wealth, sincere in-laws, a successful job, lavish house, honest friends etc. A childless couple should never think that it is a punishment for them or there is a reason for it. There is no reason for it. It is purely Allah's (SWT) distribution of His bounties, which no one can understand. Allah (SWT) put His messengers through many trials also. All His decisions are full of wisdom and only He can understand them.

May Allah (SWT) grant all of us, those with children and those without, the ability to be patient and understand

His decisions.

May He always make us aware of the objective of our creation and give us the ability to reflect on it. Oh Lord, make our children a source of solace and permanent reward for us, Ameen.

Hadhrat Abu Huraira recounts our beloved Prophet (PBUH) saying:

"There will be some people who will enter the highest ranks of Heaven. They themselves would be amazed at this because their deeds were not of the calibre to elevate them to such a level. Allah (SWT) will tell them that their children continuously prayed for them after their death. Every prayer of theirs made them exalt in ranks of Heaven, Masha'Allah."

With lots of prayers, I trust you in Allah's (SWT) protection, my child.

Your Mother,
Urfana Ayub

Letter No 43.

The treasure of my life

My child Adam Ayub
Greetings from your mother with lots of love and prayers

How are you? It is my heartiest prayer that may your grave be fragrant, airy, illuminated and one of the gardens of Heaven, Ameen.

Adam I learnt a few very important lessons after you which have helped me get close to Allah (SWT) and His people. All the things that I learned became my partners in life. Here are two duas which helped me a lot after your departure.

إِنَّ اللَّهَ مَعَ الصَّابِرِينَ *

"Surely, Allah is with those who are patient."

Surah Al-Baqarah (The Cow), 2:153

You know Adam, supplication is the essence of prayer.

إِنَّا لِلَّهِ وَإِنَّا إِلَيْهِ رَاجِعُونَ اللَّهُمَّ أَجُرْنِى فِى مُصِيبَتِى وَأَخْلِفْ لِى خَيْرًا مِنْهَا *

"Verily we belong to Allah and truly to Him shall we return. O Allah! Protect me in this calamity that has befallen me and replace it with something better"

Tirmidhi

213

These two Duas are my all-time allies. Whenever I get hurt, or my heart is grieved, or I miss you or face any trouble, these act as prayers and therapeutic medicines, praise be to Allah.

Adam, I have made it my routine to recite the prayer for forgiveness *(Dua-e-Maghfirah)*. I was not aware of this Dua before. After your departure, the teacher of my Qur'an class, Baji Naheed, came to our house for condolences. She brought a card on which this Dua was written. Since that day, all our family members, including children, have learnt this Dua by heart. We call it Adam's Dua. I pray to Allah (SWT) that, whenever we recite this Dua, or anyone else whom we have taught it reads it, let its reward also go to Baji Naheed and her family. May Allah (SWT) accept all her endeavours in the way of our religion, Ameen.

Dua-e-Maghfirah

اَللّٰهُمَّ اغْفِرْلَهَ وَارْحَمْهَ وَعَافِهِ وَاعْفُ عَنْهُ وَأَكْرِمْ نُزُلَهَ وَوَسِّعْ مُدْخَلَهَ وَاغْسِلْهُ بِالْمَآئِ وَالثَّلْجِ وَالْبَرَدِ وَنَقِّهِ مِنَ الْخَطَايَا كَمَا نَقَّيْتَ الثَّوْبَ الْأَبْيَضَ مِنَ الدَّنَسِ وَأَبْدِلْهُ دَارًا خَيْرًا مِّنْ دَارِهِ وَأَهْلاً خَيْرًا مِّنْ أَهْلِهِ وَزَوْجًا خَيْرًا مِّنْ زَوْجِهِ وَأَدْخِلْهُ الْجَنَّةَ وَأَعِذْهُ مِنْ عَذَابِ الْقَبْرِ وَ مِنْ عَذَابَ النَّارِ.

"O Allah, forgive him and have mercy on him and give him strength and pardon him. Be generous to him and cause his entrance to be wide and wash him with water and snow and hail. Cleanse him of his transgressions as a white cloth is cleansed of stains. Give him an abode better than his home, and a family better than his family and a wife better than his wife. Take him to Paradise and protect him from the punishment of the grave and from the punishment of Hellfire"

Mishkah

Another deed, which has provided a lot of peace in my life, is offering the *Nafl-e-Hajah* (Prayer for fulfilment of a need) and *Namaz-e-Istikhara* (Prayer for guidance). It is human nature to get disturbed easily and think our problems are huge. As they say

"Do not tell Allah that you are facing big problems, tell your troubles that your Allah (SWT) is the greatest of all".

The best solution to every problem is to lay your troubles before Allah (SWT) and ask for His guidance. I have made this a compulsory part of my life. Our needs are so many that we never get satisfied, but their fulfilment is entirely dependent on our Creator and Sustainer. Another thing I have learned is that sharing your troubles with people is far less helpful and productive than taking them to Allah (SWT) immediately and directly.

Our needs are of different kinds. At times two *Nafl-e-Hajah* should be offered just for mental peace and tranquillity. These have helped me a lot, Praise be to Allah .

Dua-e-Hajah

لَا إِلٰهَ إِلَّا اللهُ الْحَلِيْمُ الْكَرِيْمُ، سُبْحَانَ اللهِ رَبِّ الْعَرْشِ الْعَظِيْمِ، الْحَمْدُ للهِ رَبِّ الْعَالَمِيْنَ، اَللّٰهُمَّ إِنِّيْ أَسْأَلُكَ مُوْجِبَاتِ رَحْمَتِكَ وَعَزَائِمَ مَغْفِرَتِكَ وَالْغَنِيْمَةَ مِنْ كُلِّ بِرٍّ وَالسَّلَامَةَ مِنْ كُلِّ إِثْمٍ، لَا تَدَعْ لِيْ ذَنْبًا إِلَّا غَفَرْتَهُ وَلَا هَمًّا إِلَّا فَرَّجْتَهُ وَلَا حَاجَةً هِيَ لَكَ رِضًا إِلَّا قَضَيْتَهَا يَا أَرْحَمَ الرَّاحِمِيْنَ.

"There is no deity but Allah most forbearing, supreme in Honour. Glory be to Allah, lord of the great throne. Praise be to Allah, lord of the Universes. O Allah! I seek of you the means of (deserving) your mercy, the means of (ascertaining)

*your forgiveness, the benefit from all virtues and the freedom
from all sins. O Allah! Leave no mistake of mine without your
forgiveness, nor stress without relief, nor any need of which
you approve without being fulfilled by you, O most merciful of
the merciful"*

Tirmidhi, Ibn e Majah, Nasai

Nafal-e-Istikhara is actually seeking Allah's (SWT) will and
opinion. No soul on this earth can give you a better and
sincerer suggestion than our Creator. There is no doubt
that taking advice from good friends is beneficial, but
consulting Allah (SWT) regarding all your worries and
following His recommendations is a means of ultimate
success and blessings.

اللّهُمَّ إِنِّي أَسْتَخِيرُكَ بِعِلْمِكَ، وَأَسْتَقْدِرُكَ بِقُدْرَتِكَ، وَأَسْأَلُكَ مِنْ فَضْلِكَ الْعَظِيمِ، فَإِنَّكَ تَقْدِرُ
وَلا أَقْدِرُ، وَتَعْلَمُ وَلا أَعْلَمُ، وَأَنْتَ عَلاَّمُ الْغُيُوبِ. اللّهُمَّ إِنْ كُنْتَ تَعْلَمُ أَنَّ هَذَا الأَمْرَ خَيْرٌ
لِي فِي دِينِي وَمَعَاشِي وَعَاقِبَةِ أَمْرِي، فَاقْدُرْهُ لِي وَيَسِّرْهُ لِي، ثُمَّ بَارِكْ لِي فِيهِ، وَإِنْ كُنْتَ
تَعْلَمُ أَنَّ هَذَا الأَمْرَ شَرٌّ لِي فِي دِينِي وَمَعَاشِي وَعَاقِبَةِ أَمْرِي، فَاصْرِفْهُ عَنِّي، وَاصْرِفْنِي
عَنْهُ، وَاقْدُرْ لِي الْخَيْرَ حَيْثُ كَانَ، ثُمَّ أَرْضِنِي بِهِ.

*"O Allah! I ask guidance from Your knowledge, and power
from your might and I ask for Your great blessings. You are
capable and I am not. You know and I do not and You know
the unseen. O, Allah! If You know that this job is good for
my religion and my subsistence and in my hereafter - then
You ordain it for me and make it easy for me to get, and then
bless me in it, and if You know that this job is harmful to me
in my religion and subsistence and in the hereafter, then keep
it away from me and let me be away from it. And ordain for
the good wherever it is, and let me be content with it."*

Allah (SWT) says in Surah-e-Baqarah:

"And when My servants ask you, concerning Me - indeed I am near. I respond to the invocation of the supplicant when he calls upon me."

Surah Al-Baqarah (The Cow), 2:186

Hadhrat Abu Masood Badri (RA) quotes our beloved Prophet (PBUH) as saying, *"Whomsoever recites the last two verses of Surah-e-Baqarah at night, they will suffice for him"*

Sahih Bukhari, 4008

آمَنَ الرَّسُولُ بِمَا أُنْزِلَ إِلَيْهِ مِنْ رَبِّهِ وَالْمُؤْمِنُونَ كُلٌّ آمَنَ بِاللهِ وَمَلائِكَتِهِ وَكُتُبِهِ وَرُسُلِهِ لَا نُفَرِّقُ بَيْنَ أَحَدٍ مِنْ رُسُلِهِ وَقَالُوا سَمِعْنَا وَأَطَعْنَا غُفْرَانَكَ رَبَّنَا وَإِلَيْكَ الْمَصِيرُ لَا يُكَلِّفُ اللهُ نَفْسًا إِلَّا وُسْعَهَا لَهَا مَا كَسَبَتْ وَعَلَيْهَا مَا اكْتَسَبَتْ رَبَّنَا لَا تُؤَاخِذْنَا إِنْ نَسِينَا أَوْ أَخْطَأْنَا رَبَّنَا وَلَا تَحْمِلْ عَلَيْنَا إِصْرًا كَمَا حَمَلْتَهُ عَلَى الَّذِينَ مِنْ قَبْلِنَا رَبَّنَا وَلَا تُحَمِّلْنَا مَا لَا طَاقَةَ لَنَا بِهِ وَاعْفُ عَنَّا وَاغْفِرْ لَنَا وَارْحَمْنَا أَنْتَ مَوْلَانَا فَانْصُرْنَا عَلَى الْقَوْمِ الْكَافِرِينَ.

The Messenger has believed in what was revealed to him from his Lord, and [so have] the believers. All of them have believed in Allah and His angels and His books and His messengers, [saying], 'We make no distinction between any of His messengers'. And they say, 'We hear and we obey. [We seek] Your forgiveness, our Lord, and to You is the [final] destination'. Allah does not burden a soul except [with that within] its capacity. It will have what it has gained, and it will bear what it has earned. Our Lord, do not impose blame upon us if we have forgotten or erred. Our Lord, and lay not upon us a burden like that which You laid upon those before us. Our Lord, and not make us bear the burden which we have no ability to bear. And pardon us; and forgive us; and have mercy upon us. You are our protector, so give us victory over the disbelieving people."

I have memorised the ninety nine names of Allah (SWT) praise be to Allah and I have understood the importance of reciting these names. Allah (SWT) says in the Holy Qur'an:

"Say, 'you call upon Him saying Allah or saying Rahman (Most Affectionate) whichever you call upon, all are His good names'."

Surah Al-Isra' (The Journey by Night)/Bani Israel (Children of Israel) 17:110

Hadhrat Abu Huraira quotes our last Prophet (PBUH) as saying:

"There are ninety nine names of Allah. Anyone who memorises these names will enter heaven."

I have perceived the objective of man's creation. As Allah (SWT) says in Holy Qur'an:

"And I have created the Jinn and the humans only for this that they may worship/obey Me."

Surah Adh-Dhariyat (The Winds that Scatter), 51:56

Adam, the following is my favourite Dua, which is actually Allah's (SWT) praise recited by the angels. It is also Allah's (SWT) favourite:

سبحان الله وبحمده عدد خلقه، ورضا نفسه، وزنة عرشه، ومداد كلمات

218

equal to the number of His creations, equal to His approval,
equal to the weight of His Arsh (throne) and equal to the ink
used for writing His praise."

And of course reciting *Darood shareef* (praise of the prophet)
is a part of my routine which is also highly favoured by Allah
(SWT). Hadhrat Abi Bin Ka'ab (RA) says:

"I asked Rasul Allah (PBUH), 'O Allah's Prophet: 'I send
an abundance of Darood on you daily. How much of my
supplication time should I spend on reciting Darood?'
The Prophet (PBUH) replied, 'As much as you wish'. asked,
'Is one-fourth time sufficient?' The Prophet (PBUH) replied,
'As much as you wish, but if you spend more than this it
will be better for you'. I asked, 'Should I spend half the
time on Darood?' The Prophet (PBUH) replied, 'As you wish,
but if you exceed this time it will be better for you.' I asked,
'Then should I spend two-thirds of my supplication time?'
The Prophet (PBUH) again replied, 'As you wish, but if you
spend more time than this it will be of benefit to you'. I
said, 'I will spend my entire time of Dua on Darood', and
the Prophet (PBUH) said, 'It will suffice for all your troubles
and grievances and will be a cause of the forgiveness of
your sins'."

Tirmidhi, 2457

Adam, my daily routine of *Ibadah (worship)* is my life's
treasure. These are priceless pearls. Ever since these
prayers and *Zikr* have become an obligatory part of my
daily routine, all my worries and anxieties have been
replaced by solace, Alhamdolilah.

All this is possible only when one connects with Allah.

Every relationship requires time, service, sacrifice, love and respect. The same applies to our relationship with our Creator. Just like any other relationship, we have to prove our love and respect for Allah (SWT) also. We cannot form a connection merely by saying so, Adam. When we prostrate before Allah five times a day during Salah we very humbly offer the proof of our love.

Similarly, when we engage in *Nafli Ibadah* (optional prayer) and spend our time in Allah's *Zikr*, we are trying to prove our love for Allah.

I pray to Allah, that instead of connecting ourselves with the finite relationships of this world, may He give us the ability, wisdom and insight to connect ourselves with the everlasting and greatest of them all - a relationship with our Creator, Ameen.

We can train our children in the best possible way by connecting them with Allah. If we manage to give all the worldly goods to our children, but do not have Allah (SWT) as an important part of their lives, then we must remember that we have done a bad deed towards our children. Our children may very likely ask us on the Day of Judgment why we never connected them with Allah.

When a child starts becoming more familiar and aware of his environment and parents, he should be introduced to Allah at that time. The longer lasting our friendship with Allah; the better it will be for us.

Adam, may you be in Allah's protection and guard my child. As I am writing this letter, whenever I glance at the wardrobe in my room I can see your smiling face, where you often used to stand leaning against the cupboard.

My child, I give you in Allah's (SWT) protection.

Your Mother,
Urfana Ayub

Letter No 44.

Allah's (SWT) Wisdom and Blessings

Dear son Adam,
Who made the desert of my desolation fragrant with the beautiful flowers of your memories.

Your mother sends you her love and lots of prayers. I often think that the important incidents that occur in our lives, the different people we meet and the many places we visit are not just a coincidence. Similarly, some tasks do not get done today, but are completed tomorrow, or those people who we don't meet today may cross our paths the next day. Before, I used to view all these things as chance, but now I try to go into the depth of all such matters.

When we reflect on Allah's (SWT) decisions, then we begin to understand His wisdom. It is just like a jigsaw puzzle. When you first look at it, the pieces do not seem to fit together, but when you apply your mind to it and spend some time, it no longer remains a puzzle. It becomes a picture! If a particular task does not get done despite our efforts, then I take it that Allah does not want this task to be finished. Everything seems to be going smoothly, but obviously there was some hindrance in its way.

By the same token, if I meet someone in life who helps me in some way, then I understand that he/she was specially sent by Allah to facilitate me!

I have also learned that there is a specific time for every task. Allah fixes the time for everything. If Allah wills a

222

specific task to be completed tomorrow, then we will not be able to finish it today no matter how much we try. This authority lies with Allah only.

Adam, when I scrutinise my life, I realise that I was not aware of many of Allah's (SWT) decisions at the time they happened. It took years for me to understand them. Many of Allah's wisdoms do not become apparent to us immediately, but finally, when we do understand them, we have to bow before Him in gratitude.

If you want peace in life, then refrain from disobeying Allah. So many parents complain that their children are rude and not good to them. Adam, the truth is that when we, the parents, are disobedient to Allah, then how can we expect our children to be obedient to us?

Importantly, I now understand that we have to get connected with Allah (SWT). We humans spend our entire lives making and maintaining bonds with other people, who, in spite of all these efforts, are still not pleased and satisfied. Ironically these same people who are trying so hard are completely unaware about forming a relationship with our Sustainer.

Yet Allah is so magnanimous and forgiving that:

I sin daily
He covers it with His blessings
I can't change my habit
He is known for His benevolence

Actually, we Muslims are reaping a harvest of troubles as a result of our bad deeds and ignorance.

As a poet said:

You are facing difficulties because of your deeds
Otherwise, your troubles would have eased
You could rule the entire world O Muslim
If you understand the potentials of being a Muslim

Adam, lately I heard a very impressive lecture regarding Salah. May Allah (SWT) make this speech a source of permanent reward for its orator, Ameen. In his talk, he said that we Muslims have been offering Salah for many years. For instance, some have been offering it for the last 20 years, some for 30 years and others for 40 or even 50 years, but if a survey is conducted, it is evident that most people do not know the meaning of what they recite in Salah. Very few people understand the meaning of Arabic verses while offering Salah. The speaker gave his suggestion that if a Muslim takes leave for a week from his workplace or shuts his business for a week and spends this time on memorising and understanding the meaning of Salah, he would gain many more benefits than the loss of one week's income, Insha'Allah. In his speech he also said that people may have many worldly degrees, even Ph.D.s, but when it comes to the religious education of Muslims, most of us are ignorant about it.

Allah (SWT) has blessed us with uncountable bounties. We can never thank Him for all that He has blessed us with. If insects did not grow in the Allahowns (storage structures for wheat) and the grains did not rot, then we would have hoarded the harvest like gold and silver and let others die of hunger. Allah caused dead bodies to smell within days; otherwise, no one would bury their loved ones. And Allah grants us Sabr (patience) after troubles and difficulties, otherwise, no one would ever be free of his grievances and life would become a constant torture.

"So which of the Blessings of your Lord will you both (jinns and men) deny?"

Surah Ar-Rahman (The Most Gracious), 55:13

Adam, someone sent me this beautiful poem:
Questions and Answers

I asked how can I get your help O Lord
The answer was "Seek help through patience and Salah",
   Surah Al-Baqarah (The Cow), 2:45
I said I have sinned a lot
The answer was "Despair not of the Mercy of Allah, verily Allah forgives all sins."
   Surah Az-Zumar (The Groups), 39:53
I said my heart lacks peace and comfort
The answer was "Unquestionably the hearts are assured by the remembrance of Allah (SWT)"
   Surah Ar-Ra'd (The Thunder), 13:28
I said I am very lonely. The answer was "And We are closer to him than (his) jugular vein"
   Surah Qaf, 50:16
I said no one thinks of me. The answer was "Remember me; I will remember you"
   Surah Al-Baqarah (The Cow), 2:152

May Allah (SWT) be your guardian my child.

Your Mother, Urfana Ayub

Behavioural issues

My very loving son Adam Ayub who connected me with Allah (SWT), peace be upon you.
Lots of love and prayers.

Adam, I want to share a few things with you. Yesterday I was talking on the phone to a very dear friend of mine who had recently gotten married. I could not attend her wedding due to some other commitment. She told me that her marriage was dissolved within a few days after the event. The reason behind it was the bitter attitudes of people, which were laying the foundations of this new relationship on a basis of lies and hypocrisy.

This trend is increasing day by day. People seem very different on the outside, but their inner self is quite opposite to their exterior. They hide their interior behind beautiful coverings so effectively that you cannot see through them. In any relationship, when you come across such people, you usually distance yourself in order to be protected from their evil, but when you are married to someone like that, you face a real dilemma. Maybe my unfortunate friend also faced similar circumstances? I could not control my tears after hearing of her sorrows.

Adam, why do people act like this? Lies are bound to be revealed one day. Relationships based on deception and falsehoods are not only difficult, but in fact, almost impossible to maintain. Many people's lives around me are based on lies. These people engulf you in the snare of deceit so skilfully that you take all their stories for truth as you build your new relationship with them. Indeed the relationship can even be a strong and respectful link like Nikah (marriage contract) or a trusted friendship.

I have met many such selfish people who tell lies so fluently and with so much ease that you start wondering whether what they are saying is genuine or invented, although you are well aware of what is the truth and what is not. When I meet dishonest people I become apprehensive. At the same time, I am also worried about their hereafter. I feel sorry for them that they feel the need to tell lies for petty things which are of no benefit to anyone, not even themselves. Lying is simply a habit.

As Sayyadna Abdullah (RA) quotes our beloved Prophet (PBUH):

"Verily truth leads a man towards goodness and goodness leads to Heaven. The man keeps telling the truth until he reaches the rank of Siddique (truthful). And verily falsehood leads man towards evil and evil leads to hell. The man keeps telling lies until he is written as a 'liar' before Allah (SWT)."

Bukhari: Kitab ul Adab (Book of general behaviour): 6094

Adam, I feel that people often tell lies, because if their truth is revealed, then their worldly tasks and goals would not be fulfilled, such as establishing a new relationship with someone or doing business and trade.

Yet I am really amazed at the people who tells lies. Doesn't they ever consider that the result is at best a very temporary gain? The bright light of truth is bound to replace the temporary shadow of lies. People will ultimately come to know what is truth and what is false.

Adam, without Allah's guidance, man continues to wander in the labyrinth of ignorance. When he strays away from the right track, he lands in hell. Adam, I pray to Allah (SWT) that may He keep us away from the filth of lies. May He guide us towards the right path and give us the ability to correct our mistakes, Ameen.

Apart from lies, jealousy and greed are also fatal behavioural illnesses. Allah's (SWT) Prophet (PBUH) said,

"Imaan and jealousy cannot exist together in a person's heart"

A jealous person is disliked by Allah because he is unhappy with the fact that Allah (SWT) has granted more to someone else and not him. As Allah says in holy Qur'an:

"Or are they jealous of people for what Allah has given them of His bounty?"

Surah An-Nisa' (The Women), 4:54

Adam, this sickness develops in the hearts of people and gradually erodes them spiritually. The main concern is *"If I do not possess a particular blessing of Allah (SWT), why should anyone else have it?".* Just like a dry log is reduced to ashes after catching fire, similarly, a jealous person keeps burning in his own unhappiness and envy and finally destroys himself.

A jealous individual suffers in two ways. First, he damages himself. The poison of jealousy not only makes his speech

228

bitter, but also robs his face of its innocence and radiance. Secondly, such a person is at fault in Allah's (SWT) court, because he is not satisfied with his fate and Allah's (SWT) distribution of bounties.

Imam Ghazali says, *"Had Allah (SWT) distributed His bounties according to wisdom and intelligence, then animals and stupid people would have died of hunger. The worldly position of people entirely depends on fate, and the hereafter on hard work and perseverance, but people toil for the world and leave the hereafter to their fates."*

Jealousy does not suit humans. This is because it is the satanic trait which prevented *Iblees* (Satan) from bowing before Hadhrat Adam (AS) and turned an *Abid* (one who engages in prayers) into a cursed Satan.

Adam, another dangerous illness common in mankind is greed. Greed destroys its owner. It distances us from Allah (SWT) as well as from people. When greed enters the heart, that person's appetite for power, status and riches never gets quenched. He builds a house, but it is not grand enough, so he gets busy building a bigger house. Finally, this greed makes him oblivious to his duties towards Allah (SWT).

Sayyadna Anas (RA) quotes our beloved Prophet (PBUH) as saying,

"Man gets old, but two things thrive in him, greed and hope"

Adam, the truth is that greed keeps a man always hungry and striving for more. It makes man restless and destroys his peace. He works to increase his riches from double to treble and then to four times until finally he meets with

229

death.

As Allah (SWT) says in Holy Qur'an:

*"The mutual rivalry for piling up (riches of this world) diverts
you, until ye visit the graves"*

Surah At-Takaathur (Piling up), 102:1-2

Ironically man thinks that an abundance of worldly comfort
and riches will ensure happiness and success, but he does
not find peace. He still eats two loaves of bread and sleeps on
a bed. Often this greed makes him estranged from his near
and dear ones. When his relatives do not receive any help
and sympathy from such a greedy person in their difficult
times, they become indifferent to him and ultimately he is
left all alone.

Adam, I have closely watched the lives of many such people,
who have thriving businesses, but now reside on their own
in their luxurious mansions.

Sayyadna Ibn-e-Ka'ab bin Malik (RA) quotes his father
recounting our beloved Prophet's (PBUH) observation:

*"Two hungry wolves let loose in a flock of sheep will not
cause as much mischief and devastation as greed for money
and riches will cause in the religion of a man"*

Tirmidhi

As a poet said

People have forgotten Allah (SWT) in their quest for money

They are concerned with riches, not with its bestower

Adam, I pray that may Allah (SWT) keep everyone, including myself, in His protection and keep us away from serious faults in our behaviour, like falsehood, jealousy and greed. May He keep us satisfied with His distribution of bounties and teach us to be happy with other people's successes and happiness. May He adorn our world and our hereafter, Ameen.

May you be in Allah's (SWT) protection dear son.

Your Mum,
Urfana Ayub

The beautiful landscapes of nature

My very dear and respected son Adam.
Peace be upon you, lots of love and prayers.

How is my son? I am certain that you are well in the protection of my Lord. Adam, your Daddy and I are in Turkey's city Alanya on a short holiday. This is a hilly area, which has donned nature's very pretty clothes. The rise on which our hotel is situated overlooks the beautiful Mediterranean Sea. This lovely city has been enhanced by the majestic natural beauty of its surroundings. On one side a mountain range shelters the city and on the other side is the blue stretch of sea.

It seems as though the ocean encompasses the whole world Ma Sha Allah. This is a flawless system of Allah, which we can never comprehend! The deep blue waves and the buoyant waters testify to the greatness and might of Allah (SWT), while the golden rays of the sun reflecting off the surface produce an amazing radiance. I think I have never looked at the sea so intently before in my life. Adam, just picture it - shimmering blue sea down below and above, the endless azure sky stretched over the earth by Allah The changing colours of the sky and sea produced a stunning vista. People from all over the world visit Turkey to enjoy this exquisite scenery. Visitors from different countries, religions and cultures, who speak many different tongues - all are impressed by Allah's (SWT) creations. Of course they are all Allah's creations as well.

The comfort and peace which we experience when viewing nature's beauty are unequalled by anything else. The serenity and solace provided by the sound of the waves, the setting sun, the blue sky, the melodious waterfalls and enticing flowers can never be obtained from man-made technology.

Adam, it is for everyone to experience and test that "*water is life*". This water may be in the form of Allah's blessing, which falls from the sky or is part of a sandy beach – there to provide comfort to the bare feet walking on it. Nothing in the world can equal a sip of water.

We went up the mountains to enjoy their vistas. Masha' Allah man has very expertly carved out the rock to make space for cities and towns.

Grapevines creeping up houses built in the mountains, orchards packed with lemons, oranges and bananas and the awe-inspiring scenes of trees loaded with figs and loquat made me reflect on this verse of the Qur'an:

"And it is He who has produced gardens, trellised and untrellised, and date palms and figs in which are various kinds of food and olives and pomegranates similar in some respects and dissimilar in some other respects. Eat of its fruits when they yield and pay due thereof on the day of harvesting, and spend not wastefully. Undoubtedly, He does not like those who spend wastefully."

Surah Al-An'am (The Cattle), 6:141

Caves built in mountains are an amazing sight. These are at quite a height and are a major tourist attraction. From the outside, these mountains appear very ordinary, covered by trees and plants, but the caves within these rocky peaks provide a sign of Allah's (SWT) greatness. Just like trees have roots, mountains too have roots made of rocks and boulders which can be seen in these caves.

Do you know Adam, that mountains also praise Allah (SWT), as is mentioned in the Qur'an:

"It was Us who made the hills declare, in unison with him (Dawood), our Praises, in the afternoon and at break of day, And the birds gathered all with him did turn (to Allah)"

Surah Saad 38:18-19

It was in the peaceful and serene environment of mountains where Allah conferred prophethood on His very respected and high ranking messengers such as Prophet Muhammad (PBUH) and Hadhrat Musa (Moses) (may Allah (SWT) send his blessings upon him). To this day, anyone in search of Allah's closeness will be drawn towards this splendour. Yet hundreds of years ago, these very mountains annihilated many mutinous and insubordinate tribes and people on Allah's command. We must keep in mind too that these impressive rugged heights also warn us of the harrowing Day of Judgment when mountains will float in the air just like balls of cotton wool.

Adam, you are with me every step of this journey. I left Arslan, Ambar and Ahmad behind, but took you along on this holiday. Do you know how? I brought a photo frame containing a picture of you with your two brothers which was taken on the memorable occasion of your eighteenth birthday. A lot of my very precious memories are associated with this frame. After you, I developed a unique and emotional association with it. When you left us all and embarked on the journey to your heavenly abode, I hugged this photograph and stood crying for hours. You performed Umrah with us courtesy of this photograph. Wherever I travelled after you, you went with me in my suitcase. I may forget to pack anything else, but never you, praise be to Allah.

I strongly feel I should thank Allah (SWT) day and night for His countless blessings, praise be to Allah. He has blessed me with a healthy body, eyes, ears, nose, hands, legs and all other organs to enjoy, feel and experience all the beauty of nature wholeheartedly.

During this journey, we met a guide in a wheelchair. He told us that 15 years ago one of his legs was damaged in a motorcycle accident which left him disabled. His eyes filled with tears as he narrated this incident to us. No doubt every organ of ours is a supreme gift from Allah, praise be to Allah.

It is Allah's blessing that Masha'Allah he has blessed man with a computer-like mind, which when used beneficially enables him to reflect and meditate on the universe and solve many problems. Adam, the truth is that the computer's invention was inspired by none other than the human mind! All its different parts, like software, hardware, memory disc, were engineered on the basis of the human brain. But a computer cannot compete with the human mind. The computer is just a robot, which neither has emotions nor can it operate without a programme. On the other hand, Masha' Allah, Allah (SWT) has blessed man with the very superior gift of an intelligent brain, but alas, either we do not use it properly or do not use it enough.

For example something which pains me, Adam, is the heartless waste of food in hotels. This is not unique to hotels and restaurants, but in many homes too, everywhere, in every country. When we eat buffet meals, then we automatically take the liberty to dump as much food in the dustbin as we like. We have paid for it, so it is our property. For this reason, people fill plates to overflowing, but eat a small portion only. All the rest is wasted. Allah (SWT) has commanded us to observe moderation in everything and He has forbidden us to waste food.

Our beloved Prophet (PBUH) said:

"Live simply, observe moderation, be healthy"

Mishkah

Regarding moderation in food our Prophet (PBUH) said:

"A Momin (a believer) fills one gut while eating and a Kafir (disbeliever) fills seven guts while eating"

Tirmidhi

The bitter truth is that half the world is dying of hunger today. They do not have access to pure drinking water, food is in short supply, and innocent children are dying because of famine. One part of humanity is crying due to hunger and the other is dieting to lose weight. Adam, we must all obey Allah's command that we respect food and be moderate in eating.

Adam, I wish that in Muslim countries, or in Muslim hotels

and restaurants, all customers (Muslim and non-Muslim) would be trained to drink water while sitting and in three separate breaths. They should be given information from Sunnah and science to support these teachings. Qur'anic verses and The Prophet's (PBUH) sayings condemning the waste of food should be displayed in all eateries and people made aware of the fact that Allah (SWT) dislikes wastage of food. Maybe some of us will learn from it. Many people do not even know that it is a sin to waste food.

I have found that it is difficult to identify many Muslims as such just on the basis of their actions. When they speak, the use of words such as *Asalaam alaykum* (peace be upon you), Insha'Allah, Masha'Allah tells others that they are Muslims. But when a Muslim tries to imitate other religions and cultures in order to be accepted there, then he loses his own identity. A true Muslim (adopt) only *"Allah's (SWT) shade"*. *Sibgatullah* (Colour of Allah) is a very enduring hue, which never fades. No other colour can cover it. A Muslim may go to any corner of the world and the colour remains true.

As Allah says in the glorious Qur'an:

"Our life takes its hue from Allah! And who could give a better hue than Allah?, and we are worshippers of Him."

Surah Al-Baqarah (The Cow), 2:138

I pray Adam that the whole Ummah of Prophet Muhammad (PBUH), including me, may be covered by Allah's colour and may He make us indifferent to all other colours.
As a poet said

I am your servant, Oh Lord
Colour me in your shade, Oh Lord
Let me be like fragrance
Which is confined within your hand, Oh Lord
Let me benefit by your remembrance
Let me lose myself in you, Oh Lord
You are with me every step of the way
Colour me in your shade, Oh Lord

May you be in Allah's (SWT) protection my child.

Your Mother,
Urfana Ayub

The weather has kind of changed

My very dear son Adam Ayub, lots of love and prayers from my heart.

Adam, I am feeling very depressed today. My heart is desolate. It seems as if I am standing alone in a desert where there is no living soul, no sign of life at all. Time seems to have stood still. There is complete silence and loneliness. Although when I look around me, everything is there, but this sense of anguish and melancholy seems to be gobbling up any trace of happiness, leaving me feeling like dead leaves.

What a contrast of environment I feel! Outside, the weather is so delightful and exuberant, but when the inside weather is sorrowful, then desolate emotions of the heart have the upper hand.

Adam, I have told you this before, but I want to share my feelings again. I am amazed by the fact that when my life passes through important or landmark dates, then everything associated with that date - people, places and events - comes to mind and I feel the loss more keenly. Even if time has moulded a person into a very strong and brave individual, still some days, months or occasions unwillingly push one into the past. What surprises me is, how does the heart know? Is there a calendar inside it which tells it about these dates?

The weather has kind of changed

The weather has kind of changed since you departed
Neither is the season same nor am I
Why has the weather changed?
Your memories grieve me, they make me cry
A strange feeling has surrounded my heart
The weather has kind of changed since you departed
How my heart pines to have you back
Your memories grieve me and make me cry
Now you live in my dreams and memories
The truth is that the weather has kind of changed
I can't find you in this changed world
My heart longs to hear your footsteps,
the weather has kind of changed
Another year has passed by
Time passes and the weather has kind of changed
Outside all the seasons are as before
But the season of my heart has kind of changed
The weather has kind of changed since you departed
Neither the season is the same nor me
It seems that the changed season
Has managed to change me too
(Urfana Ayub)

I have been missing you intensely for the last few days. Do you know why? because it is your birthday tomorrow. In the world of my heart, you will be 24 years old Masha'Allah. It was my desire to see you as an adult, to get you married soon and become a young granny. Had you been alive, all this might have been possible. Adam, when I began to understand our religion, I came to know that Allah (SWT) does not like words such as *"if"* and *"if only"*, because they produce a feeling of longing in man. The best way to cope: whatever situation we face, may Allah teach us to be satisfied with His will.

الحمد لله علىٰ كل حال

"I thank Allah in every situation"

As a poet said:

Stars were flying in air last night
As I sat lonely with my Allah
Teach me how to make my Duas fulfilled
Or make me be content with your will
(Ameen)

I have offered *Nafil-e-Hajah* (prayer of need) just now and prayed for my patience and your *Maghfirah* (forgiveness). Supplication is truly a Momin's weapon. When a person prays with full sincerity of the heart, then Allah does not let him go empty-handed. Our beloved Prophet (PBUH) said:

"Your Sustainer is very Modest and Magnanimous. When His servants stretch out their arms to Him in prayer He feels ashamed to let them return empty handed"

Ibn-e-Majah

Adam, giving *Sadaqa* (charity) is very satisfying. Allah makes the heart content with it. Our beloved Prophet (PBUH) said:

"Any one of you who gives a single date from his (fair) income as Sadaqa, it will be taken by Allah (SWT) in His right hand. Allah only accepts fair income. He makes the money given in Sadaqa

grow and prosper as a man rears and nurtures his calf, until
that charity becomes the size of a mountain"

Bukhari

Abu Huraira quotes our Prophet Muhammad (PBUH) as saying:

"Deeds which make a Momin continue to receive Allah's
blessings even after his death are; the knowledge which he
imparted to others and spread it around, the pious children
which he left behind, the Holy Qur'an which he left behind as
inheritance, a mosque which he built, a rest area which he
constructed for passengers, a canal which he had made and
the Sadaqa which he gave from his income during his healthy
days in life. All these will be a source of reward for the person
even after his death"

Ibn-e-Majah

I pray to Allah (SWT) Adam to make our hands *"giving hands"*
and may He provide us with sufficient time, money and
resources to fulfill our charitable aims. Ever since I have
started giving Sadqa and feeding the birds Masha'Allah,
I feel that Allah helps me in unseen ways and allows my
money to go further to bring benefits. Many people do not
fully comprehend the meanings of the word *Barakah* (flow
of blessing from Allah. I feel that *Barakah* is magic which
we do not understand. We can't touch it with our hands,
but can feel and appreciate it in our hearts.

Hadhrat Abu Huraira (RA) quotes our Prophet Muhammad
(PBUH) as saying:

"No day passes when two angels are not sent down from

242

Allah (SWT). One of them prays for a person who spends his money and says, 'O Lord give a good return for his money to this spender'. The second angel curses the stingy people and says, 'O Allah (SWT) ruin this miserly person.'"

Muslim

Adam, I pray that may Allah grant generosity of spirit within our hearts so that we spend money given by Allah (SWT) in His name, Ameen. Allah has big rewards for people who spend for His cause.

"Those who spend their wealth (in Allah's way) by night and by day, secretly and publicly - they will have their reward with their Lord. And no fear will there be concerning them, nor will they grieve."

Surah Al-Baqarah (The Cow), 2:274

I started writing this letter yesterday, but could not complete it. Today is 7th May, your birthday. Masha'Allah you are 24 years old in the world of my heart. Everybody thought and talked about you today.

Adam, few years ago birthdays meant a great deal to me, but as I gained insight, I realised that with each passing year our lifespan is actually decreasing. We have less remaining time at our disposal before we die. Now these things seem meaningless. Every year people celebrate birthdays and New Year with great zeal without understanding that time is flying by and one brick has been removed from their life's building with each passing year. This is a matter of concern for everyone, not celebration. The fact that we have less

243

remaining time should be food for thought. Are we fully packed for our journey?

What is life?

Life is a delicate thread	*let not this thread sever*
Life is a china doll	*let not this doll shatter*
Life is a beautiful dream	*let not this dream shatter*
Life is a breath of air	*let not this breath pass away*
Life is a drop of rain	*let not this drop fall*
Life is an enchanting moment	*let not this moment fade*

This life is like a thread
Which is bound to sever

Life is like porcelain china	*which is bound to break*
Life is like a dream	*which is bound to shatter*
Life is a breath of air	*which is bound to pass away*
Life is a drop of rain	*which is bound to fall*
Life is a moment	*which is bound to pass away*

I realized the meaning of life Adam
When I saw you wrapped in white Kafan
You are made of mud

You are buried in mud
This is the truth of life
This is the reality of life
If only we can understand it
We know it but do not accept it

(Urfana Ayub)

Dear child may you be in Allah's protection.

Your Mother,
Urfana Ayub

Letter No 48.

Our parents, our paradise

My child Muhammad Adam Ayub, who is the reason for me to meet many extraordinary people in this world. Peace be upon you.

I want to share some happy news with you. Masha'Allah, my parents, your Nani Ammi and Nana Abbu, are coming to England to meet us for the first time since your departure from this world. The reason behind this long gap was partly Nana Abbu's illness. Last year he fell seriously ill. His recovery was almost like getting a new life. Praise be to Allah , now he has finally agreed to come over to meet his children and his brother and sister-in-law.

I feel as if they are coming to England for the first time, although they have been here many times before to see us. Maybe this is so because this will be their first visit after you and they will meet you at your final abode.

Adam, parents are our Heaven. Their presence is like cool shadows. Just like a shady tree which provides relief from scorching sun, parents and their prayers protect children from the ups and downs of life and keep them safe.

Sayyadna Abbu Umama (RA) quotes in Ibn-e-Majah,

"A person asked our Prophet (PBUH), 'O Rasool Allah (Prophet of Allah) what is the right of parents over their children?' The Prophet (PBUH) replied, 'Your parents are your Heaven and they are your hell.'"

246

Adam, man can succeed both in this world and the hereafter by serving his parents. Hadhrat Anas (RA) quotes our Prophet (PBUH) as saying,

"Anyone who wants longevity in life and expanse in his money should be good to his parents and mend relations"

Al Targheeb wal Tarbeeb

Allah (SWT) has encouraged us to be good and humane with our parents, Subhan'Allah. Allah (SWT) says in Qur'an:

"And do good unto [your] parents"

Surah Al-Isra' (The Journey by Night)/Bani Israel (Children of Israel) 17:23

Adam, if we keep our parents pleased and happy they will pray for their children, but if the parents are unhappy with the children, then the children will not find peace either in this world or in the hereafter. I think mental peace is the highest rank of happiness one can attain.

Parents' prayers work like magic. The emotion and devotion found in the prayers of parents cannot be matched by any other relationship.

As someone aptly said:

Who showers prayers on me I wonder?
The sea throws me out whenever I tend to sink
Adam, often this blind love for their children creates trouble for the parents. Most parents face this situation

when their children are no longer theirs alone, but get involved in other relationships ordained by Allah (SWT). Now a child becomes someone's husband, or wife and daughter-in-law or son-in-law. One of the many bad trends spreading in our society is the ill-treatment of the daughter-in-law. This lack of respect is responsible for the extreme degree of tension seen in many homes nowadays. I believe the main reason for this cruel behaviour stems from ignorance towards our religion.

The glorious Qur'an describes everyone's rights in detail and sets out the hierarchy in relationships. It tells us of the reward we will get if we honour others' rights, and also the fate of unjust people. But Adam, it seems as though we follow our own rules and regulations in our homes rather than Allah's (SWT) rules, and thus continue to trample on others' rights.

I feel that, before bringing someone's daughter into one's home and becoming a mother-in-law, every mother must prepare herself mentally for the fact that her son will not remain only her son anymore; he will be someone's husband too. Soon he will be involved in fatherhood and all the other relationships with his in-laws. Adam, I have seen very good and obedient sons suffer due to their parents' demands on one side and their wives' wishes on the other. This conflict destroys the peace of the house.

Islam lays stress on the *"family system"*. A society is formed by people living together in harmony. When families share ties of love and respect with one another, then a peaceful society will come into existence Insha'Allah.

But today, a daughter-in-law does not want to look at her mother and sister-in-law, a mother-in-law does not speak to her daughter-in-law; distances keep increasing and finally this hatred is transferred to the next generation. Some sons and daughters-in-law respect their own parents, but not the parents of their spouses.

Adam, parents are parents, whether they are parents of a son or a daughter. Allah (SWT) has blessed all parents with respect. However, our society gives more respect to the son's parents. The result is that sometimes a son does not fulfil his wife's rights due to undue obedience towards his parents. Other times he fails to give his parents their due rights because of blind love for his wife.

Adam, I have come across many depressing examples of poor relationships between parents and children. Instinctively I pray, *"O Allah (SWT) give us the ability to fulfil the rights of all our relatives whether parents, children or any other"*. This is because every relationship demands rights. We must try to do justice to each of our relatives as guided by Allah (SWT), because we are going to return to Him one day and then we will be answerable for our actions.

Allah (SWT) commands us to mend and maintain blood ties. He has made every one of us different from the other. Our attitudes, thought processes everything is unique. Just think, if siblings with the same parents, brought up in the same house, do not possess similar habits or mindsets, how is it possible to expect that girls and boys married into our family will be like us? Likewise, how is it possible that your spouse's parents will share an identical way of thinking to your own parents? This is simply not possible! We tend to forget that what every person learns from his or her home, parents, environment and circumstances becomes a part of his being and reflected in his or hers personality. We cannot change it.

When there are differences in thought processes, and outlooks on life do not match, but the relationship remains very strong and solid, then we simply cannot sever the ties. We have to pull along together. In such a situation, the only option left is *Silah e Rehmi* which means mending and maintaining blood relations.

Our Prophet Muhammad (PBUH) said:

"Allah says 'I am Allah and I am Rahman (the most merciful). I created Raham (relation) a relation and named it on my name (Rahman). Now whosoever mends it, I will mend him and whosoever severs it I will sever him too'."

Tirmidhi, 1907

Adam, it is not easy to be big-hearted and mend relationships, but Allah (SWT) has promised huge rewards for doing so. We must try to get along with those family members around us who are difficult to please and bring them along with us no matter how difficult the journey is. Severing bonds is easy. Like if a part of body is afflicted with a dangerous disease, it is easy to cut it off to save the life. Similarly it is easier to cut off relationships with difficult people and much more painful to maintain them, but Adam, we must keep in mind that this pain will reap huge rewards from Allah (SWT).

Allah (SWT) has commanded in Qur'an to uphold family ties,

thus forbidding us to sever them. Our beloved Prophet (PBUH) said,

"No sin is worse than injustice and severing of relations for which Allah (SWT) admonishes in this world and also keeps in store the torture in the hereafter"

Sunan ibn e Majah, 4211

Adam, I am afraid of hardheartedness. I do not understand how people can be heartless. We must keep praying that Allah (SWT) may keep our hearts receptive. Sayyedna Abu Farash Salma (RA) quotes our Prophet (PBUH) as saying:

"If anyone breaks relations with his (Muslim) brother for one year, then this gesture is equal to shedding the blood of his brother"

Sunan Abi Daud, 4915

Adam, we must all assess ourselves and try to identify our mistakes. We expect others to give us our rights, which they should. Children should fulfil their obligation towards their parents. This is their duty, not any gratefulness. Parents too must fulfil their duty towards children, because both parents and children are answerable to Allah (SWT).

The truth is that children can never compete with their parents for their sacrifice and knowledge. Children are bound to err and take immature decisions, but if parents manage them with sensitivity, insight and courage, they will be able to keep the family together; otherwise it takes no time to shatter the relationships.

Adam, whenever I think of the family system, I am reminded of a necklace made of precious pearls. Children are like the pearls and this necklace is in the possession of parents. Parents have got the experience, wisdom, knowledge and common sense to keep this necklace intact. That is why this duty of keeping children safely linked is laid on parents. Even if this necklace tends to break, parents will not let it scatter.

It is my heartiest prayer Adam that may Allah (SWT) keeps our necklace intact. May He grant all our parents a long life, Imaan and life without any disability. May their prayers always keep shelter over us, Ameen.

May Allah (SWT) grant perception and ability to all children to respect and serve their parents in the best possible manner so that they can earn their place in Heaven. Our Prophet (PBUH) said,

"That person will not enter paradise who is insubordinate to parents, drinks alcohol and who reminds others of the favours he has done for them"

Nasai

Adam, just as children are an asset for the parents, my parents are an asset for me. By parents, I not only mean my biological parents, but also your father's parents - Ayub's mother and father, through whom I got such a wonderful husband. He is their son, Praise be to Allah . May Allah (SWT) give us the ability to give as much respect to our spouse's parents as we give to our own. May He grant wisdom to parents to treat their sons and daughters-in-law as their own children and pardon them for any mistakes they commit. Let the parents have the same principles for their own and others' children.

Adam, I like the following supplication very much. It is the children's duty to keep praying for their parents and become a source of permanent reward for them. After Allah's (SWT) grace, we get most of our advantages in life through the endeavours and sacrifices of our parents, like respect, our good name, a home, inheritance, education and status in life. Parents become a cause for your respect. For instance people still know me as Ishaque and Zahida's daughter and Yaqoob and Kulsoom's daughter-in-law. My respect is enhanced because of their names, praise be to Allah (SWT).

"My Lor * رَّبِّ ارْحَمْهُمَا كَمَا رَبَّيَانِي صَغِيرًا *? when I was small."*

Surah Al-Isra (The Journey by Night)/Bani Israel (Children of Israel) 17:24

It is my heartiest prayer that may Allah (SWT) grant my and Ayub's parents health, Imaan and life without any *mohtaji* (dependence). We can never repay them for what they have done for us. No matter how much children do for their parents, they can never repay the parents' debt.

Adam I bid farewell to you with this Dua:

"O Rabb! Inspire me to render thanks for Your favours, which You have bestowed on me and on my parents, to do such good deeds that will please You; and admit me, by Your mercy,

among Your righteous servants."

Surah An-Naml (The Ants), 27:19

Ameen.

May Allah (SWT) be your guardian Adam.

Your Mother,
Urfana Ayub

Letter No 49.

Children's marriages

Very dear son Adam, Assalam o Alaikum.

Adam, today I want to tell you something which worries me from time to time. I firmly believe that parents' love is the best of all gifts for their children. Parents try their level best to fulfil all their children's demands. Some parents even go to the extent of earning money by illegal means to fulfil the children's wishes, because for them the biggest success in life is the accomplishment of their children's dreams. Parents spend their time and money getting their children's favourite food, clothes, toys, all other paraphernalia, and organising excursions too, for their youngsters from a very young age. They try to do more than they can manage or afford. They take loans and neglect their own selves to educate their family. But when it comes to their children getting married, then Adam, most parents in our community do not grow out of their old customs and traditions.

By this I mean that the majority of traditional parents are resolved not to marry their children out of family or caste. The strict custom of marrying children within the extended family or tribe can pose problems, and at times can weaken or completely sever these ties of love between parents and children.

In such situations, if a child tells his or her parents of their choice or suggestion regarding a future life partner, then parents and others label them as *"rebellious"*.

I have had a chance to meet parents who sacrifice their children's love for the sake of their own siblings. Many parents want to marry their children into their brother's or sister's family even if the children are not a good match mentally or academically for each other.

I have also seen instances where the father and mother want to get their children married into their own respective families. This can lead to differences between the spouses which can increase to such an extent that the parents' own relationship is jeopardised. In most of these situations the children are neither consulted nor their choices taken into account, and they are not given the right to take decisions on their own either.

There is increased unease and tension in our society and the growing rate of domestic conflict is an important contributor. Adam, I do not think that any child wants to leave his/her home and relatives, but if the circumstances deteriorate to such an extent; then the child has no option left but to take extreme measures. These impossible dilemmas trap young people in a maze of confusion. On one side are their parents' love and lifelong sacrifices, and on the other is the parents' insensitivity towards their children's happiness; especially when the situation involves family complexities or a blind following of tradition.

Adam, severed relationships are very painful, no matter whose mistake it is or what the reason may be. By this I do not mean that children should not give importance to their parents' decisions, or that they should act purely on their own will and become rebels. It is a child's duty to obey his or her parents, not to offend them and try to keep them happy under all circumstances. This way they will keep benefiting from their parents' prayers as well. The Qur'an instructs children not to even wince or say 'uff before their parents.

I wish all parents would understand that our destiny lies with Allah (SWT). We have no power over it.

As a poet said:

All the strings are in your control Oh Lord
What can a puppet do?

But maybe we are under the wrong impression that we can wield some control. The fact is - one gets connected (married) only where his destiny leads. This relation is ordained by Allah (SWT), not us. Yes I believe that we all want to stay linked with our brothers and sisters because Allah (SWT) puts great stress on forging relationships.

Prophet Muhammad (PBUH) said:

"He who severs relations will not enter Heaven"

Bukhari, 5894

If there are good matches for children within the family and the children also agree to it, then nothing can be better than this. But if there is an appropriate match in a decent Muslim family outside our relatives, and our children are also inclined towards it, then parents must consider it seriously. For some people, marrying out of family is like an iron wall which can never be broken or traversed.

They do not pay heed to the fact that many girls keep ageing because of these man-made barriers and pass their marriageable age. In some families many children remain unmarried only because a suitable match within the caste or tribe was never found.

The problem does not stop here. It becomes more serious when these young people fall prey to psychiatric illnesses. The primary causes are criticism by people, pressure from society, loneliness and a sense of deprivation. This particularly applies to young women who become depressed when their dreams of a happy married life are not fulfilled. In some cases individuals can end up suffering from psychosis.

Adam, I wish I could plead with these parents:

"Please pay attention to Allah's (SWT) command and the Prophet's (PBUH) way of life. Please fulfil this very important obligation regarding your children."

It is against Allah's (SWT) orders to look for a special tribe, colour, country or tradition when seeking out life partners for our children. The first condition regarding such matters is finding a Muslim from a respectable family. It does not make any difference whether the person in question is a Gujrati, Mirpuri, or a resident of Karachi or Bengal. The main thing is that he/she should have faith in one Allah (SWT). Our beloved Prophet (PBUH) said:

"When you plan to marry a woman, take four things into consideration: 1) wealth, 2) family background, 3) beauty,

258

and 4) religion (her following thereof)."

Bukhari

Many parents do not even consider some very suitable matches which they might come across. This can lead to strained relationships between parents and children. Hatred creeps in, and often children marry independently by their own choice without taking their parents' blessings.

Parents' consent and blessings bring joy and peace for their children. How nice it would be if everyone could participate with joy in these happy occasions and give Dua's to the married couple so that Allah's (SWT) bounties pour on them like rain.

Adam, I pray that whatever relationships we are in, whether as parents or children, let us handle these in the best possible way. Let not our decisions be influenced by our ego, society, fashion, family or tribe. Let us make decisions according to Allah's (SWT) commands.

With lots of prayers, I entrust you into Allah's (SWT) protection.

Your Mother,
Urfana Ayub

Letter No 50.

Devastation by new technology and search for success

Very dear son Muhammad Adam Ayub,
Assalam o Alaikum.

I wanted to share something with you. Technology has given rise to many troubles. The widespread use has perverted our society to such an extent that the technology has become an evil in itself.

Today, the unprincipled and careless use of Facebook, WhatsApp and many other social networks is turning lives upside down. By this Adam, I do not mean that their entire use is wrong, but their unethical use is definitely not desired. Nowadays people have made life naked due to this technology, where nothing is left hidden behind a curtain of decency and social and behavioural morals have been cast aside. Personal details of all kinds of situations are available for anyone to access.

I feel as if some people have put every aspect of their lives on show where anyone can read it. There is no prohibition on anyone. Some people have restricted this information to their circle of friends only, but even between friends problems can arise. For instance, some of their friends may not have as much wealth, or achievements, or material goods. So when they see Facebook posts showing off expensive designer clothes and branded goods, or displaying photos from holidays all around the world; just imagine what longing people will feel who cannot fulfil such dreams.

Adam, everyone's heart is not so accepting. Even if they are sincerely happy for their friends, they do have desires of their own. They would also like to wear expensive clothes or be tourists in different countries.

Adam, most people now keep contact via social media rather than visiting each other. And nowadays children's ability to meet people and converse with them is decreasing due to these internet connections.

Here all sorts of domestic news is posted along with photos. Now the news of the whole family and the world can be received through Facebook. Many people come to know about important events like the birth of a baby via these Facebook pictures. At the same time this can cause problems in an already strained relationship, for instance: *"Nobody told us about that news. We got to know it via Facebook."* Almost as though Facebook were a *"city reporter"*.

Jealousy is a well-documented human trait, Adam. So when people yearn for something, it is also possible that they fall victim to a curse.

What's more, where many loving friends are present, there are bound to be a few enemies too. Why not protect ourselves from them? But people do not understand this point and neglect such thoughts as being old-fashioned. Adam, I am not concerned about others' thinking, but I believe one's intentions must be true and sincere. I feel that my life should never be a source of yearning for anyone, because I would never like to hurt anyone's feelings, whether friend or stranger, deliberately or unknowingly.

Our ancestors rightly observed, *"Riches and women should be kept veiled"*. Exhibiting riches can be a cause of mischief, whereas a woman definitely is *mastoor,* that is, a *"hidden thing"*.

Actually all these social media interactions are leisure activities. Satan exhausts our abilities and time through very attractive diversions. Yet our bodies, minds, heart, eyes and spirit all need nurturing. Today our bodies are lazy, with little ability to work because they are not provided with appropriate diet and exercise. Most households make use of fast food, because the constant use of technology leaves one with very little free time. Our minds are entangled in the problems of this world all the time, while our hearts are filled with its glamour which has become a fulltime resident. We are slaves of our desires. Instead of us controlling our desires, our desires control us. We do not know what is meant by purity of spirit.

Adam, none of the new inventions are bad per se. These are signs of developed nations whom Allah (SWT) has blessed with so much knowledge and success. But we must take care not to lose ourselves in these new inventions. We must never be ignorant of our Creator. When we are sitting before our laptops or tablets, we must never ignore the Salah timings and the fact that Allah (SWT) is calling us towards success. That success which we all want to attain and which will never diminish, but we have forgotten the way to it. We all want to succeed, but we keep wasting hours and hours of our time.

Adam, I want to ask people, *"Is there anyone who does not want to succeed in this world?"* Even without actually asking, I know that there won't be many *'No'* answers, because it is human nature for everyone to want success in life.

I have an answer for all these people. The prescription for success is the *Muazzan's* (prayer caller) call for prayer which is given five times a day; the Adhan which keeps summoning people towards success.

Translation of Adhan (call for prayer):

Allah is the Greatest, Allah is the Greatest, Allah is the Greatest, Allah is the Greatest
I testify that there is no true deity but Allah
I testify that there is no true deity but Allah
I testify that Muhammad (PBUH) is Allah's Prophet
I testify that Muhammad (PBUH) is Allah's Prophet
Come towards Salah, come towards Salah
Come towards success, come towards success
Allah is the Greatest, Allah is the Greatest
There is no true deity but Allah

Adam I wish that everyone, including myself, would understand that Allah is the greatest of all, and no technology or social media engagement is important enough that we lose the remembrance of our Sustainer for it!

May you be in Allah's (SWT) protection my child.

Your Mother,
Urfana Ayub

Letter No 51.

The conviction of birds

My extremely dear and very sincere friend Adam,
Assalam o Alaikum.

I am experiencing a strange feeling. It seems as though I
am going to be separated from you once again. These letters
provided a strong association with you. All the things that
I wanted to share with you I wrote in these letters. I know
you will not be able to read them, but because of you, my
message will reach a lot of people, as these letters will be
gathered together into a book *"My letters to You"* for
publication. I hope and pray that people read my letters to
you with understanding and perception.

Adam, Praise be to Allah, *"My Letters to You"* has reached its
final stage and will be published soon by the Grace of Allah
(SWT). I have got into the habit of meeting you continuously
by way of these letters. But now that I know this book is
nearing completion, I feel depressed. It is my prayer that
may Allah (SWT) keep all of our intentions, especially mine,
sincere towards His will and may He shower His blessings
upon this project, Ameen. Let this book evoke thinking and
meditation in its readers and strengthen our Imaan and
trust in Allah (SWT) so it is just like that of the birds.

Bullhay Shah has beautifully described it:

Look at the flying birds Oh man
Just look at what they do
Neither do they hoard food

Nor do they die of hunger
Has anyone seen birds dying of hunger?
It is the man who hoards food and he is the one who dies of
hunger (undoubtedly)

May Allah (SWT) give us so much faith that we do not even think of committing sin and may He give us the belief that our Creator is watching over us at all times.

As a poet said:

The thought of sin would simply fade from this world
If we believe that Allah (SWT) is watching

Adam, with each passing day I am also becoming more aware that being careful with one's tongue is a very challenging task. It is more difficult than safeguarding our money and belongings. Birds get trapped because of their claws, fish because of their mouth, cattle because of their feet and man falls into traps because of his tongue!

The words uttered by our tongue can elevate us to great heights, but on the other hand, a man's speech is also responsible for pulling him down to earth. Our speech is very powerful. It can make us loved and respected or it can degrade a man to a subhuman level. Words are under the control of their master before they are spoken, but after uttering them man becomes a slave of his spoken words.

May Allah (SWT) give us all, including me, the ability and power to keep our tongues under control. May He make us choose our words with care and give softness to our speech. Our words sometimes insult others and cause many hearts to break. Allah (SWT) has blessed man with a mind and intellect so that he can use it in a positive manner instead of reproaching others.

As a poet said:

> Man is the one who treats another man like a beggar
> There is no poverty in Allah's blessings

Lots of love my child.

Your Mother,
Urfana Ayub

Letter No 52.

The "few people"

My son Muhammad Adam Ayub,
Assalam o Alaikum.

Adam, my heart is very unhappy today. Do you know why? The day which we used to talk about so much came and passed yesterday. It was our silver jubilee wedding anniversary. Praise be to Allah, it seems those 25 years passed in the blink of an eye, but this blink changed my life completely. Many colours and seasons came into my life during this time. The most attractive of all these colours was your existance which entered my life soon after my marriage praise be to Allah. It made me your mother at a very tender age. When you reached the age at which I had become your mother, you left this world forever.

My relationship with you is not broken, Adam, but it is no longer there for the world to see. However, the connection between our hearts has grown with each passing day.

Yesterday, I missed you a lot. My eyes kept seeking you and wanted to cry. Though you were not there Adam, but your Nana Abba, Nani Ammi, Dada Abbu and Dadi Ammi's prayers were with me praise be to Allah. Significant days and dates are very important in our lives. All the memories associated with these landmark days are also very valuable. I remembered all that we used to say about this day. Praise be to Allah it was a very pleasant day filled with emotions of happiness, gratitude and sorrow which passed peacefully, just like other days.

Adam, there is something that I have realised very acutely today. Sometimes we are engrossed in our life's joys so much that we do not understand another person's sorrow. This action of ours is often unintentional. We are so lost in the whirlpools of our own lives that we are unable to perceive others' grief.

Another lesson that I have learnt from life is that when you are in pain, seek another person who is in pain or trouble and try to help alleviate his problems. Insha'Allah this good deed will help you in your difficulties. So, when in pain, try to understand others' struggles. I have also realised that problems enhance when mentioned or discussed, decrease when one remains silent, vanish when you persevere in keeping with Allah's will, and are replaced by happiness when you thank Allah, Masha'Allah.

I wish that Allah (SWT) may grant me with such wisdom and patience and strengthen my Imaan. Someone has very wisely observed that Imaan is like an airplane. The higher it ascends, the smaller the world seems.

Adam, I pray for my good behaviour. This is Allah's (SWT) best reward, because tenderness and good behaviour are languages which even the blind and deaf can understand.

Some people spend their entire lives earning money with dishonesty, shrewdness and no concern for others, but they forget that there will be no pockets or cabinets in their Kafan to store these riches.

It is my fervent prayer that may Allah (SWT) give us the ability to do good deeds because it is said that those who do good will gain light. May Allah (SWT) grant us the understanding of religious as well as worldly knowledge so that we may succeed in the world and the hereafter, Ameen.

Once Hadhrat Umar (RA) passed a man who was praying, *"Oh Allah (SWT)! Include me in Your few chosen people, Oh Allah (SWT)! Include me in Your few chosen people."*

Hadhrat Umar asked him where he had learnt that dua. He replied,

"From Allah's (SWT) book because Allah (SWT) says in the Qur'an: "And there are but a few thankful ones among my servants."

Surah Saba (Sheba), 34:13

When Hadhrat Umar heard this, he began to cry and admonished himself by saying, *"Oh Umar! People are more knowledgeable than you. Oh Lord! Include me in Your few people as well."*

The Qur'an refers to *"most people"* as those who do not know, do not thank, do not accept Islam, are disobedient, uncivilised, who stray away from the right path, who do not think and do not listen!

Come, let's include ourselves in the *"few people"*, even if we are left all alone in this world's race!

It is my prayer to Allah.

As a poet said:

Before the world gets a chance to humiliate me
Oh Allah! heal my body and my soul
I am responsible for this condition of mine
Make me as You want me to be
Let my decisions be based on Your approval
May Your command be my wish

(Ameen)

With lots of prayers for my Adam.

Your Mother,
Urfana Ayub

Letter No 53.

Karachi Heat

Dear son Adam, Assalam o Alaikum.

Today, a friend's father died. He was in Pakistan and had been ill for some time. My friend was planning to go to Pakistan next month to see him. She was very upset and grieved at not being able to meet him before death. Undoubtedly Adam, every event, programme and time of everything has been fixed, which is solely in the power of Allah (SWT). Incidents like these force me to think that we cannot do anything even if we want to. This friend of mine wanted to meet her sick father in Pakistan. She had bought air tickets for travel next month, but she could not go because it was not Allah's will. The apparent reason for it could be anything. In contrast, some other siblings and relatives who were not planning to go reached there after hearing the news. All such things make us realise that we are simply puppets who cannot move without Allah's command.

I remember when my elder *Khala* (aunty) died, my cousin was coming from abroad to see his mother. Khala died just a few minutes before her son could reach the hospital from the airport. These occurrences become a cause for yearning *"that I could not reach her despite reaching Pakistan"*. Even though he reached Pakistan, he could not see his mother alive.

It is my prayer that may Allah never let us face such a situation which will become a pain and longing for the rest of our lives.

Adam, do you remember I told you that Nana Abu and Nani Ammi are coming to England to meet you? Out of the blue, I had to go to Karachi for an important task and I returned to UK with them. All of this was Allah's (SWT) wisdom. Otherwise, I was not planning to go to Pakistan this year.

This time the weather in Karachi was extremely hot. The weather of Pakistan is usually hot, but this year temperatures broke the records held for many years. The heat was so intense, it felt as if the sun had come closer to the earth. Sweltering winds, hot water coming from the taps, constant sweating; even the air conditioner did not provide much relief. The fans seemed to blow out hot air only.

Within a few days, many people died in Karachi due to the heat wave. I heard that there was a shortage of ambulances to transport the dead bodies because of the alarming number of deaths.

Adam, for the first time I got really scared of the heat of hellfire. I know that the heat of the hereafter bears no comparison to this world's heat, but how scorching hot that would be? Will we be able to endure it? This was a very alarming thought.

Adam, I feel that as time passes, the sincerity and love which was seen in people before is not seen anymore. Life has become very business-like. This is more so in cities, where there is usually a lot of rushing about and things going on and the world seems very selfish. The trends of society also change with time. I like Bashir Badar's poem, which captures the feelings of my heart:

Strange is the life of the city, it is neither travel nor stay
A business-like afternoon and an unpleasant night
No more are there the blessings of prayers, the advice and
instructions
Sincerity out of necessity and greetings on demand
Desire to meet daily, the sophisticated talk
This decency is not without reason, he wants something from
you.

(Bashir Badar)

With lots of prayers.

Your Mother,
Urfana Ayub

Letter No 54.

Aaji Ji

My friend and dear son Muhammad Adam Ayub, who revealed to me the real colour of life.
Assalam o Alaikum.

How is my child? I know the answer to this question very well, because I am only your mother who gave birth to you, whereas our Lord is our Creator whose love is more than that of seventy mothers. I know very well that you are happy and peaceful in the blessings of my Allah (SWT), praise be to Allah (SWT) .

Adam, this book is nearing its completion now. While writing these letters I have fallen into a habit of talking to you. If Allah (SWT) wills, I will connect with you again via my writings some other time in life.

Adam, my friend, I wish that people receive some benefit from these letters of mine. These are not ordinary letters to you; I hope that they become a source of guidance for others. People may see the positive aspect of life after reading this book. They may meditate on the teachings of Allah and his Prophet (PBUH). They may take decisions in life based only on the commands of Allah and not directed by the customs and traditions of society. Most important of all, people may evaluate themselves and try to find out their mistakes before criticising anyone else.

Praise be to Allah, it is the extreme benevolence of Allah (SWT) that after summoning you back, He chose me for this work and considered me appropriate for the task. Otherwise, I have neither the talent nor ability to write anything. Thank you Adam, for making Allah (SWT) choose me for this job. I pray from the core of my heart that every person who buys or reads this book gains some benefit out of it. If anyone spreads the message of this book to others or performs good deeds as a result of reading it, let it become a source of permanent reward (*Sadaqa e Jariya*) for you, me, my parents, my family members, relatives and of course the buyer/reader, Ameen.

Whenever I think of permanent reward, thousands of beautiful lamps alight in my thoughts. Just like one candle can light many other candles; similarly one act of kindness will become a cause of many other such acts, praise be to Allah. Adam, *"My Letters To You"* will act as *Sadaqa e Jariya* for you. All the income from this book will be used for social work Insha'Allah so that buyers and readers may also participate in good deeds by choosing this book.

Adam I told you that your Nana Abu and Nani Ammi are in England these days. After staying with me for a few weeks, now they are planning to go to Mamoon's house in London from where they will return to Pakistan. These few weeks passed very quickly indeed. Both of them went to meet you in the graveyard many times during their stay.

I came to see you yesterday. Whenever I think about the span of your life, I feel as if you just came and went away, whereas your parents and grandparents are still alive Masha'Allah.

As a poet said:

When you came Adhan was called and prayer was offered
when you left
Within such a short time, you came and went

Yesterday, as I was leaving after meeting you, I saw a grave with this couplet written on it:

Oh people! Recite Fatiha before going away
You will be desperate for this Dua before long

When I read this, Adam, I stood still thinking that tomorrow, when I am here in need of this prayer, how many people will pause to recite Fatiha for me? How helpless man will be at this stage. Everyone will be in dire need of prayers.

As a poet said:

You will be forced to leave this finite world one day
Everyone is helpless before Allah's command

I am proud to be the daughter of that father who thanked his Creator under all circumstances. Every single time I talk to Abbu Ji on the phone and ask how he is, do you know what his answer is? *"Alhamdolilah! Thanks to my Creator, everything is peaceful due to His benevolence and kindness. How are you, my child?"*

Adam, last year when Abbu Ji fell seriously ill and was fighting for his life, even then his answer was the same. I am thankful to Allah (SWT) for blessing him with health and life.

No doubt parents are a priceless gift of Allah (SWT). A son had his elderly mother admitted to a nursing home because he could not look after her. He used to visit her on and off. When the mother was about to die, she called her son for a final meeting. The son asked, *"Do you have any last wish that I can fulfil?"*

The mother replied, *"Son, get the fans of this nursing home changed. It is very hot and they do not work properly."*

The son was surprised on his mother's last wish and said, *"What benefit will you get from the new fans?"* She said, *"My life has passed, but I am worried for you, son. When your children leave you here, how will you tolerate this heat?"*

Adam, this is an example of a mother's selfless love!

I wish and pray that no matter how much this world changes, let our values remain consistent, that we may never forget to respect our parents and elders and care for our children. Let us keep our children connected to their maternal and paternal families so that they can collect the true love of these relationships and perceive their sweetness.

Ties of blood are very strong. Sometimes we may become distant from family because of temporary strife, but their pain grieves us and their joys make us happy. I remember the days of my childhood when my Nani Ammi was alive. We used to go to her house for every summer holidays and meet the whole family. All the relatives used to pour love and attention on us. Praise be to Allah Adam we are very lucky people to be surrounded by such loving relatives. Not everyone is blessed with these bounties. We must always value these relationships.

Adam, this morning when Nana Abba woke up, I asked him, *"Abbu Ji, did you sleep well last night?"*

"No," he replied, and the reason for this was that he kept remembering and missing his Aaji Ji (my Dada Abbu). He kept thinking about his father all night. For a moment, I was a bit surprised that Abbu Ji was missing his Aaji Ji. But I was amazed at my own thoughts. Parents are parents. No matter what age one reaches, parents' loss is felt by everyone.

Abbu Ji told us that my Dada Abbu was very hospitable. An example of his generosity is that, if there were no guests at the house on any particular day, he would bring home random people from the railway station and offer food to them. He was man of his principles. If he said anything, he would stick to it and respect that promise and others respected him for it. He was an extremely decent and hardworking man. While Abbu Ji was narrating all this, I was trying to read his face expression.

Memories are a great resource for anybody. You can take them out whenever you want to and then store them safely again. They belong to us only. No one can take them away. Adam, I feel that your memories are with me at all times.

As a poet said:

How can I get rid of his memories?
He is present on every road of my thoughts
I was telling you how friendly my Aaji Ji (Dada Abbu) was. Nana Abbu told me that once that a girl's Baraat (future

bridegroom and his wedding party) came to the village one week before the wedding due to some misunderstanding. The girl's family said that the marriage would be held on the date that had been fixed and asked the groom's family to go home. But the Baraat had come from far away and it was difficult for them to return. My Dada Abbu made arrangements for the Baraat to stay at his house for one week. He catered for them in every way and finally the ceremony took place on the designated day.

Adam, now our attitudes are such that we are very quick to defame others' daughters. Yet my Aaji Ji acted as host for a girl's marriage party for one week, treating them to the same hospitality as if the bride were his own daughter. We do not see such values anymore these days. These are our traditions, which we must honour. If we put these traditions into practice, Allah (SWT) will bless us with respect too, Insha'Allah.

As the time for Ammi and Abbu's departure for Pakistan draws close, I am forced to think that it is true that daughters cannot remain with their parents forever. They get married and move to their husbands' houses, but sons can remain close to their parents if they wish to. Those sons and daughters-in-law are lucky who get a chance to live with their parents, because parents' prayers shield them from evil all the time.

Adam, for the first time I felt envy for Mamoon Atif, Aunty Fozia and their children that Allah (SWT) chose for them to live with my parents. Every one of us has a different fate. People move away from their parents due to jobs or migration abroad. Daughters, despite wanting to, cannot maintain the same closeness to their parents after marriage that sons and daughters-in-law can. No doubt parents' prayers are the same for all their children, but it is also true, Adam, that those children who live with their parents and serve them, take the bulk of their parents' blessings, praise be to Allah (SWT) .

All my prayers are with those children who live with their parents, look after them and earn their prayers, thus improving their world and hereafter. We must realise that this is a very good bargain. A daughter-in-law can also very efficiently fulfil her obligation because Allah (SWT) has given her a chance to serve their husband's parents who are now her parents as well. Adam, if a girl takes blessings from her in-laws by attending to them, it is my staunch belief that her own parents will also get a sincere daughter-in-law who will assist them and get their blessings. And in time, she herself will get a good daughter-in-law Insha'Allah.

As a poet said:

It is much easier to care for children than your parents
This point I understood very late in life

Adam, now that I have finished this discussion regarding children and parents' relations, I entrust you to my glorious Rabb. As I near the completion of this series of letters to you, I do so with full trust and hope in Allah (SWT). It is my prayer from the core of my heart that may Allah (SWT) give uncountable goodness and expanse to *"My Letters To You"*, Ameen.

Allah Hafiz

My child, my friend and my teacher in this world and hereafter,

Your Mother
Urfana Ayub

Letter No 55.

My letter for my parents, (Ammi and Abbu Ji)

My son and my very sincere friend who made me understand life's relationships, Muhammad Adam Ayub. Assalam o Alaikum.

Adam, you are well aware that this book and all the letters written in it are addressed to you, my child. But this last letter I am dedicating to your Nana Abbu and Nani Ammi.

My very respected Abbu Ji and my beloved Ammi Ji, Assalam o Alaikum.

Ammi Ji, I want to dedicate a poem to you which represents the sentiments of my heart.

Mother

You are the essence of my breath, the name of my fragrance
You are my esteem and through you I got respect
Every prayer your lips utter reaches the sky
All the time I pray for your happiness and joy
Your blessings and prayers are a ticket to Heaven
Your curse seals the fate forever
I wish to serve you my whole life
I ask for your love morn' and night
Every pain of mine upsets you
How can I ever thank you?
When you see even a glimpse of pain in my eyes

You do not rest and slumber leaves your eyes
I wish I can fulfil all your dreams
And hold your sorrows' streams
Oh Lord! Let my mother's prayers be with me forever
Let her love keep shield on me forever
(Ameen)

(Urfana Ayub)

I am very lucky that you both came here to meet me. Allah (SWT) blessed you with health so that you could endure such a long journey, Masha'Allah. It gives me so much happiness when I come to meet you in Pakistan, but every daughter wishes to have her parents visit her at her house too. This time you came after a long gap and praise be to Allah stayed for nearly five weeks with me. After you went away, my house and my heart both became desolate. I miss your shelter. I miss your love and affection very much. I cannot thank my Lord enough for all the beautiful memories which you left here at my house. These memories brought back many joyful recollections of my childhood and now I have new memories from this time too.

Abbu Ji, after you left I wanted to see you sitting on the chair where you always used to sit. I look for your water bottle and glass on the table. This morning when I came in the TV lounge, your chair was vacant. My eyes kept seeking you in the empty room, but I could not find you. I wanted to hear your voice returning my greetings. Instinctively, I greeted myself and then responded in your manner.

Abbu Ji, my story of love and affection revolves around you. May Allah (SWT) keep your shelter over me always and may He grant you with complete health, a strong Imaan and a long life, Ameen.

Ammi Ji, my eyes wanted to see you walking across the lawn. For a moment, the thought crossed my mind that maybe you're still there reciting the Kalimah, as was your routine, and making the trees, shrubs and grass a witness to it. But you were not there. May Allah (SWT) make this action of yours *Sadaqa e Jariya* for you, Ameen.

As a poet said:

> *Tell me O, Mother! who will write with her lips after you*
> *A prayer on my forehead when it's time to leave*

My eyes were filled with tears as I bade farewell to you, but after you departed I became very restless. I had a feeling of suffocation. That is why Allah (SWT) has made the parental relationship so sweet that no other connection in this wide world can match it. Similarly, no one else on earth can replace the sincerity, love and prayers of parents. Only parents' love is a hundred percent pure and completely selfless.

As a poet said:

> *When someone asks me where one can find love?*
> *I smile and think of you, Mum and Dad*

Undoubtedly, a mother's love and a father's affection are the best of Allah's (SWT) gifts. Praise be to Allah I am proud to be a daughter of yours. Both of you possess the best of characters and values. There are very few people like you these days. You gave me your full and unconditional love and a superb childhood. I do not mean that other parents do not do so much for their children, but I believe that very few have the heart to shower as much love and respect on their daughter as you have done.

I want to tell you through this book, *"My Letters To You"*, that I love you both very much. I always thought I was close to my mother as daughters usually are, but the realities of practical living have proved that I was your reflection, Abbu Ji. Mostly children never tell their parents how much they love them. I think we should express our devotion to all our loved ones.

It is my heartfelt prayer that may Allah (SWT) always keep your shade of protection over us. May your doors be always open for us. People say that the doors of their parents' house are open for their daughters only while the parents live. Afterwards, the situation changes. I feel very grieved when I hear about this happening. It is my contention that after the parents die, brothers and sisters-in-law (Bhabhis) must be large-hearted enough to accommodate the daughters so that they can visit their parents' house without inhibition. I firmly believe that if Bhabhis treat their sisters-in-law (Nands) with love and respect, then Insha'Allah their Bhabhis will also keep their doors open for them.

Abbu Ji, every daughter is a Nand somewhere and a Bhabhi elsewhere. When she is fair with others, they will treat her well. I pray that may Allah (SWT) give all brothers the substance to keep their hearts and houses open for their sisters, Ameen.

No doubt our parents are a source of respect for us. Their status, character and money bring their children honour and respect. By the same token, good, decent children reflect well on their parents and this creates wider esteem. These relationships are tied to each other in that each bestows respect on the other in the eyes of the community.

Praise be to Allah, by the grace of Allah (SWT) and your prayers I have come across very loving and sincere people in my life who gave me a lot of respect. I think it is a great blessing of Allah (SWT) that people bestow their love on you. Whenever we receive this blessing, we must remember that we did not earn it; it is purely Allah's (SWT) benevolence that He made us a focus for people's love. If we do not value this love, then just like any other bounty, Allah (SWT) can erase affection for us from the hearts of people.

As a poet said:

> *People of the world love me*
> *It is because of my mother's prayers*
>
> **(Niazi)**

Just as in our previous visits, you both taught me many things.

Abbu Ji, you say:

> *"Excess of anything is harmful."*
> *"Open and read the Qur'an daily may it be only one page."*
> *"Offer Salah early in its stipulated time."*
> *"Respect your parents and love the children."*
> *"When you keep your Rabb pleased, He will grant you everything. So always be mindful of His commands and never go against them."*

And Ammi Ji, I will never forget the advice you gave when leaving:

"I know you respect Baji and Bhai (parents-in-law) a lot and serve them too, but I think you must do more. Serve them with all your heart and take their blessings. Parents' prayers can change a man's fate. They are your parents now; do not even give them cause to complain."

This was followed by further priceless advice, *"There is no give and take with parents. Parents do not expect or want anything from children. One should give them the best one has, only for Allah's (SWT) sake, without thinking what they would give in return."*

Praise be to Allah it is all your teaching. I do not take any credit for it. From the day that I entered this household after marriage, I have treated Ammi, Abbu and all the family members with full sincerity of heart. I don't know whether I have been able to please them or not, but my mind is fully satisfied. Insha'Allah I will be able to stand before Allah (SWT) with a peaceful heart. I pray to Allah (SWT) to keep my intentions pure and keep me in the protection of prayers always, Ameen.

Ammi and Abbu Ji, I also believe that *"what goes round comes around"*. How I behave towards the children's Dada and Dadi today will come back to me tomorrow. Our problem is that we forget that what we sow today, we reap later. Our deeds will come back to us in this world as well as in the hereafter.

I end this letter with the wish and prayer that may Allah (SWT) keep you both together in His protection and grant you with a long life. Abbu Ji, may you always enjoy the company of your queen, and Ammi Ji, may you always have Abbu's protection over you. May Allah (SWT) bring you both back to us with health, happiness and strength of Imaan and may you distribute your love and prayers amongst us again, Ameen.

I pray that Allah (SWT) grants us the ability to treat our parents-in-law in the best possible manner.

While children must understand that, even if they have higher academic degrees and their parents are uneducated, their elders still have many *"honorary degrees"* on the basis of their experience. We can never disregard their knowledge, actions, experience and wisdom. After all, parents are parents. I pray that may all the parents enjoy a life of health without any *muhtaji* (dependence), may they remain mobile and be able to recite Kalimah when departing from this world, Ameen.

I entrust you both to the protection of my exalted Rabb

Allah Hafiz.

Your Daughter, Your Urfi,
Urfana Ayub

Letters for Adam,
from his family and friends

The apple of my eye, Adam Ayub
Assalam o Alaikum O residents of graves.

I hope that you are well and peaceful in the blessings of Allah (SWT).

More than five years have passed since you left this world. Sometimes it feels that centuries have passed since you parted from us. At times it seems that you never parted and sometimes I feel that you are here with us. My child, there are many sentiments and feelings in our memories, love, happiness and sorrow, which are difficult to explain, convey or write down; they can only be felt.

What I have to say is very concise
Living without you is not easy

I remember every moment of the last time when you came to stay with us in Karachi (Pakistan) and all your previous visits as well. The last time when you were with us your health improved considerably. You were very happy then and wanted to prolong your stay. You visited Punjab, Kashmir and many other places and met all the relatives. You stayed with Mamoon Kashif and went to Murree (A hill station in the North Western part of Pakistan) which you enjoyed a lot. You also went for Umrah and visited Allah's (SWT) house and the Prophet's (PBUH) mosque, but who could have guessed that it was my last meeting with my child? I fondly remember how you used to love everyone, respect the elders and care for the children.

Your memory is so intense,
it went to extremes by crossing every limit

When you came last time, you liked eating almonds. I was afraid that almonds might not be good for your health because you had a heart problem. That is why I used to say, *"Son, do not eat more than 5-6 almonds at one time"*. Now this pinches my conscience. Had I known that it was your last food from my house, I would've let you eat as much as you liked. As a poet said:

My relation with you is spiritual not verbal
You are present in my breath like a perfume

Dear child, your Nana Abu and I are coming to the UK to meet you. Previously, whenever we went to your house, you always came to greet us at the airport. You used to be very happy and gave a lot of respect to us. We always saw you in the temporary house of this world, but this time we are coming to meet you in your eternal abode. I understand that meeting you like this will be difficult for us and will require a lot of patience, but the truth is that from now on we will have to come to meet you like that. May Allah (SWT) grant us the courage and ability to see you like this.

I remember I phoned you the day you separated from us. You picked up the phone and said, *"Nani please pray for me. I have pain in my stomach. I am not feeling well and my appetite is gone."* We had talked for quite some time, but I did not know then that it would be my last conversation with you. Otherwise, I would have talked a lot more, but I am thankful to Allah (SWT) that I heard your voice and conversed with you on your last day in this world. As I am writing this letter to you, I can imagine you standing before me smiling and looking at me. You are saying something to me which, though I cannot hear, I can still perceive.

I miss you very much. You were, and still are, my first grandson and very dear to me. My dear child, love and relationships do not die or end, but they do diminish or get separated by Allah's (SWT) will. We all are subordinate to His will. We practice patience and thank Him. I pray to the benevolent Allah (SWT) for you and all the Muslims. As a poet said:

From sin, I could not part
But you never broke my heart
I tried to seal my fate with hell
But Your magnanimity did not let me

Oh Allah (SWT), give my child Adam and all the Muslims a life of respect and death of martyrdom (Shahadah). Let us all recite Kalimah at the time of our death and make us enter Heaven. Make our graves bright and let Heaven's window open in them. Oh Lord, give our deeds record in our right hand and keep us steadfast on *Pul Siraat*. Resurrect us as the Ummah of Prophet Muhammad (PBUH) and give us a place near his feet. Save us from the mischief of *Dajjal* (Antichrist) and give us a peaceful death. Let us be in control of our minds and bodies till death. Do not let us be dependent on others and let us all meet together in Jannat-ul-Firdous, Ameen.

Dear son, you parted from us due to stomach ache. We plead to our Lord that He may give you the rank of a *Shaheed* (Martyr), Ameen.

You are lucky my boy that you are remembered by your own people as well as strangers. This is all because of your own goodness and all the work that your parents are doing for your eternal reward. Otherwise, many people are such that, in the words of this poet:

They buried you and went away without any niceties
What has happened to the world in such a short time?

It happens that people forget the dead ones very quickly after their departure, but we all remember and miss you. Your mother has written a book for you which will be a source of permanent reward for you. May Allah (SWT) make this project easy for her, Ameen. First she wrote a book *"After You Were Gone"* and now she is working on *"My Letters To You"*. May Allah (SWT) grant expanse in her endeavours because she is doing all this work for your *Maghfirah* (forgiveness). I pray that may Allah (SWT) accept these ventures, be pleased with her, forgive her and grant her bounties befitting to His grace, Ameen. It is my heartiest prayers that may Allah (SWT) forgive your sins or any other mistakes committed due to human weakness by His grace.

I pray that may Allah (SWT) give the record of our deeds in our right hand on the Day of Judgement and let us recite the *Kalimah* at the time of our death, Ameen. May He prevent our souls from wandering and give us abode in a high place. May He make our graves wide and illuminated and grant us and you the food of Heaven, Ameen. As a poet said:

Let me love you so much Oh my Lord
That I may recite Kalimah at my last breath

Allah Hafiz
Lots of prayers from your Nana Abu Muhammad
Ishaque and Nani Ammi Zahida Nasreen (Maternal
Grandparents)

293

Dear Adam, Assalam o Alaikum.

I believe that our exalted and magnanimous Lord would have you in the highest ranks of Heaven Insha'Allah, Ameen.

It was very distressing to see you leave in front of my eyes, but it made me realise the truth of life. I had never understood life before or realised that its journey would be so short. Now I am scared that life can part ways with me at any time. I have understood the importance of religion in our lives and now I pay more attention to myself and my children regarding religion. I try to do everything only for Allah (SWT).

You would be happy to know that, on your mother's encouragement, I have started a programme of teaching Qur'an (Dars) at my place. I am trying to understand Qur'an myself. May Allah (SWT) give us the ability to spend our lives according to its commands, Ameen.

Your departure from this world is a big void for us, but I feel that it has led to many positive changes in our lives and has focused our attention on our Deen (religion). The reward for all the changes shall go to you, Insha'Allah.

I pray to Allah (SWT) that He may elevate you in ranks and give you a place in *Jannat-ul-Firdous*, Ameen. May Allah (SWT) give the best reward to your parents in this world and the hereafter for their patience in these difficult times.

Your Mumani,
Erum Asif

Dearest Adam,

AsalamuAlaikum WaRahmatullahi WaBarakatuh, Insha'Allah I pray that you are all in the best of health and Imaan, Ameen.

I have had a few reflective days and I wanted to share a poem with you all that definitely gave me food for thought. The root of my reflective thoughts stems from memories of my oldest nephew/son, Mohammad Adam Ayub, may he be granted the highest of heavens, Ameen. It was 4 years ago that he passed away on the 27th of December and you know Alhumdililah as a family we have made massive progress in taking the very best of life lessons from this loss, and I am sure with more learning Insha'Allah to come.

As a family we are really trying to stay away from ritualistic behaviour that doesn't comply with the Sunnah. However at certain times in the year you do definitely review, reflect and think back to stages and periods in time. I guess for me that was the case for the past few days. I am sure many of you reading this have gone through your own losses, parents, siblings, partners, children, friends, teachers, etc and it's hard, it's really hard to bear that. We all do belong to Allah (SWT) and we will return, and with that return, there is some hardship and pain for those left behind without doubt. What you make of that experience is a very individual journey, with some people transforming and others sadly breaking. I feel blessed beyond measure that this void in my life has helped me to see the Dunya (worldly life) more clearly and helped me to understand my purpose and role in this world.

I think about Adam all the time and he has motivated me in such a way that I don't think anyone or any other experience can come close. I think about where he is now and pray that he is at peace and without any pain, illness or discomfort Insha'Allah. We all see death around us, but the day to day living isn't always easy. We get easily distracted, we find a new focus and what we use to fear becomes forgotten frighteningly.

I am use to holding certain feelings and thoughts in my heart, it seems easier to deal with but today I wanted to share a few things with you all. Please really value your time, make the most of every relationship you have and honour the rights of your loved ones inshaAllah. Don't put off things for another day, seize the moment and be the best you can be today and every day InshaAllah. Ask for forgiveness from your Lord and ask him to be your eternal companion and guide, with his light and mercy you will never fall astray InshaAllah. Have faith that in every hardship InshaAllah there is ease, don't lose hope InshaAllah ease is very close by. Be kind to your parents, your neighbours and leave a positive legacy behind, happy memories, happy people and InshaAllah a happier world because of your short existence.

Forgive me if it feels like I am sharing random thoughts today. I just had these things rushing around in my head and wanted to share them. Adam was the eldest nephew and the first grandchild of the house. For me I became an aunt at the age of 10 and that was such a beautiful stage in my life Alhumdililah. I can't imagine a life without Adam, a son to me inshaAllah he will always be. Memories and people do live in the heart, but as believers we know there is a hereafter for a joyous reunion which should motivate us beyond measure.

I pray Adam my son you are in peace, you are protected and safeguarded against all difficulties and I pray we do meet Insha'Allah in *Jannut Al-Firdaus* one day, Ameen. I make the same Dua for all those reading who have also encountered loss in their lives.

Duas and Salaam

Farhat (Phuphie)

ADAM'S SMILE

All I can see is that cheeky smiling face of yours wondering through the room,

Delicately aiming for the kitchen cupboards, in order to then joyfully consume.

After all that searching, you'd get some Almond biscuits, a drink and comfortably sit down,

Make some time for Dadi Ammi and Baba. Have a chat and often remove their frowns.

So much time you had for all even the maniac kids and for that you deserve a big crown!

Smile you did, laugh you did, enjoy you did, and plenty of love to all you gave.

My memories of you are so many and so happy, and throughout it all, I think how brave.

I won't lie it hurts that you're not here to see or to hold, to hug, to call or even talk to.

Listening to each other's pain and joy reminds me to put on my smile and not to be blue.

Everlasting duas I have for you, my son, my ray of hope, my Adam just know......I do love you.

(Farhat – Adam's phuphie)

AsalamuAlaikum WaRahmatullahi WaBarakatuh,

In sha Allah I pray that you are all in the best of health and Imam, Ameen.

Today's quote is a favourite of mine. I always feel the strength of its meaning every time I read it, Alhamdulilah. This quote is something I must admit I try reflect on in-terms of my own life - although I do have to battle with it sometimes. We can have particular stages, or incidents, or people or losses in our lives where the idea that it's a 'miracle' seems very unlikely or a distant possibility, because we are so wrapped up in the distraction of all the negatives, even if they are not true. One such example I can draw on is from my own life and today seems a very good day to mention it. My eldest nephew Mohammed Adam Ayub was born on the 7th of May - 22 years ago. He was the first grandchild of the house. Masha'Allah he was like a miracle, a gift like no other and his presence, his love, his care, his mercy, his contagious smile, his laughter, his ability to bring people together and much more, all of this was a miracle Masha' Allah.

It's a blessing when a person in your life can remind you and connect you to some many people, experiences and strengths, that you feel without them it would not be possible. My whole family had this very deep, sincere and unconditional connection with Adam, very hard to explain but it was very beautiful in its nature, it could soften the hardest of hearts, Alhamdulilah. He is physically no longer with us now and he has returned back to His Maker, his rightful place. It was an exceptionally hard and challenging time when he left us, but it was so strange what happened afterwards. When you think of gifts, like your eyesight, your legs, your job, your friends, your clothes, car etc - you think of them existing in this world. You see them, you can touch them, you can do all this and more, and that verifies the existence of that thing and you can assure yourself that gift exists, it's from Allah swt. However we encountered something different. The gift of Adam came to us Masha'Allah 22 years ago, he passed away on the 27th of December 2009, yet his love, his care, his mercy, his ability to bring people together and much more still exists in this world Alhamdulilah - to this very day. He is such a beautiful soul that he never left us, he carefully, diligently and lovingly worked on all the family, rebuilding, strengthening, challenging, improving and safe-guarding us all. He in many ways helped to wake us up.

Today I feel like Adam is one of the most present souls in my life, even with him returning back to Allah swt. All the good that he did in the world, for the 18 years and 7 months he existed, have not vanished or been forgotten. I still see his friends around and how some of them have deeply been affected by his going and have come closer to their Lord, how his grave is still visited Masha'Allah by so many, the charity that is in his name still grows strong and is helping so so many people, how we as a family (and wider family) understand the fragility of our existence, but with more respect and consideration, value our life and how it impacts on others. The list can go and on.

I am writing this because we are all encouraged to remember our blessings, our gifts from Allah swt and often times we don't always think of those that have left us as gifts, or at least present gifts that still perform miracles every day. For me both Adams parents, my brother and sister in-law are 2 such miracles that I witness all the time. They have the loss of their son to endure, but have they complained, have they fought against this reality? have they challenged their fate? Alhamdulilah no, not at all. They took this stage in their life with deep grief and sorrow, but equally also with beautiful strength and might, increase in their Imaan, improved Taqwa, stronger love of their Maker and I am sure much more that I can't explain. I see them, and I think Suban'Allah after all of this, they keep going, they don't lose heart or hope and even though their son is physically not with them. That's a miracle and May Allah swt continue to protect my brother and sister in-law always, Ameen. Adam's presence has never left us and Insha'Allah for as long as that remains the gift of Adam, the miracle of Adam will stay with us - and for that Allah swt we can't thank you enough.

Duas and Salaam,
Farhat

"There are only two ways to live your life. One is as though nothing is a miracle. The other is as though everything is a miracle."

Albert Einstein

AssalamuAlaikum Wa Rahmatullahi Wa Barakatuh,

Insha'Allah I pray that you are all in the best of health and Imaan, Ameen.

I wanted to share this beautiful quote with you today because it deeply struck a chord for me. I think often in life, especially when things are not going right, or we have some kind of trauma, loss, the automatic response often is to support that person, to talk to them, find the right words to lift their spirits and mood, and this approach can work sometimes. It is what most of us do.

Then there are those moments in life where honestly no words can come close to lightening the pain that one may feel in their heart. The kind words of comfort that are shared, are usually well meant, but don't seem to really sink in, or we fail to grasp the connection. I have been in similar situations where life really throws a mighty challenge at you and it really destabilises everything. Your reality changes in every which way and nothing said by others can ever fix it or heal it. Then in and amongst all of that unrest, a loved one just being with you in silence, their loving presence, absent of words - can fill your heart with a level of peace that has a very powerful affect. That unspoken connection creates a beautiful space where not only hearts feel less heavier but they also feel connected and transformed.

I feel like today of all days this reminder seems very fitting. My nephew Mohammed Adam Ayub, May he be granted the highest ranks of heavens, ameen. Passed away 5 years ago. Time just seems to have raced ahead, and our calendars just keep clocking up, day after day after day, until years pass.

I try my hardest to move forward with the gift of life that Allah (SWT) has blessed me with. I have distracted myself with work, voluntary work, family, home, friends etc - so that I can keep focused on existing in this world. Then comes those particular occasions where you can't fight your emotions anymore, it's too tiring. Your heart just aches and hurts and you give in. Then tears fall and you remember this loss that has changed your world. In those times, in those painful seconds, that well timed pause from someone you care about is all that you need. All that is necessary Insha'Allah for you to take one step forward, rather than backwards. You really can't put a price on how special that is.

I want to thank all those souls in my life that have been generous and kind enough to give me their time, support, duas, love and their silences. You will never know truly how much it has helped me to find the strength and courage to not to just get on with life, but to 'be' in the world as an instrument of good I pray. It's all from Allah swt the choices and challenges we face, there is no accident in this.

If I can request that you keep my nephew in your duas, as well as every other soul who has passed away on this earth and those that have people to pray for them and those that don't.

Duas and Salaam,
Farhat (Adam's Phuphie)

The right word may be effective, but no word was ever as effective as a rightly timed pause.

(Mark Twain)

Dear Adam,

How do I even begin this letter to you? I have no idea really where to start from. The last 5 years seem like 50 years, and yet at the same time, it feels like only yesterday you were amongst us in this busy and distracting world.

I picture who I was on the 27th of December 5 years ago. And my mind finds it hard to remember how that 'phopie' has now become me. You know when you left that morning to go back to your Maker; I can honestly say that time stood still. I felt nothing moved or changed or existed on that day.

I just know that we'd lost you and that pain of that your departure, was deeper and more painful than anything I've ever felt in my life. It took all the strength that I had, than borrowing more from Allah swt to just survive and keep the family going. I can't recall at that time what I did in the world and of what benefit it was. But I know what I tried to do in our homes, and with the family. I tried to find a way to keep us all strong, to make sure your departure in no way was forgotten, but at the same time we accepted it and embraced it, for all the good that was intended. It's amazing how you temporarily leaving us could be seen as a blessing and a mercy, but in honesty it was and still remains the case.

I think having got very unwell after your leaving us, and having sciatica it left me in a very dark and lonely place. I had this hole in my heart and in my life, and I had to figure out some way of moving forward, of trying to reconnect back to the world. I realise I couldn't do it by myself. I'd lost strength and I felt it wasn't easy to show how vulnerable I was to the family. How could I? They needed all that I had to stay anchored themselves.

Something did help with that pain, that anguish and suffering, and that was going on the intended Umrah that we'd plan to do as a family. Despite my health being so bad, not being able to walk, bend, prostrate, get changed properly even, etc. I realised that going to Umrah was part of a life plan I couldn't ignore. People often get excited and so passionate about making plans to go to Makkah, to visit Allah swt house and I just felt scared and worried.

I didn't know if I could do everything that was obligated

upon me, which didn't leave me in a good state – my health had never been that bad before. I did however try my hardest to leave my heart as open as it could be. I just wanted to let this pilgrimage 'be' whatever it needed to be.

I remember when we left for this journey, on that first day, dressed in my white shalwaar Kameeze and getting to Manchester airport, and finding out that the connection to London was late due to bad weather, meant that we missed our original flight to Saudi. It was actually then Adam, that moment when we ran to the plane in London Heathrow and were told we couldn't board, I felt a pain in my heart. The news actually left me feeling distressed and I actually didn't realise how much I wanted and needed to get on that plane to visit Allah (SWT) house, until it got taken away from me. It was like my head and heart woke up.

I can't explain properly what I felt when I eventually got to Makkah. Just walking those blessed streets, approaching the Masjid Haram Shareef in the very early hours of the morning, it was like a cool breeze hitting your skin on a very hot night. There was something so beautiful and mesmerizing about that whole first night, seeing everything for the first time, all of it.

Your mum bless her had already completed her Umrah in the day and was exceptionally tired. Yet despite all that, she took me and Chacha Yousaf and Abid through all the stages of the Umrah. The first glance of the Kabah, the first tawaf, and the first saee - just the spiritual response to all of that, it was like I had been sleeping my whole life and that night I woke up, the light in my soul came on, the deepest part of my 'being' woke up and I never ever anticipated that happening. I remember clearly I hadn't prostrated in six months and your mum offered me a stool to sit on, to pray my two rakah nafal to complete my Umrah. I refused and said I would complete my Umrah properly and finish all the necessary actions, which I tried to do, so I prostrated during those two rakahs. Adam it was so healing, all that pain in life I had felt for so many years, the scars and wounds of traumas passed, the black hole that had taken some hold of my life, all that disappeared that night. I felt healed, soothed and even mended. Mended in such a way, that it was not back to the old popie, because she had gone. My heart had been polished and cleaned and the immense feeling of peace that I felt entering Allah (SWT) house, it lifted my being, my imaan to the heavens and above.

Your death, my first Umrah, all these were transformative moments in my life. These experiences shifted the scales in me and my moral compass was now working at a much higher level. This reminded me of what my direction of travel truly needs to be and that I need to do all that I can to keep walking that path, no matter how many distractions I come across.

Since that experience, wow Masha'Allah so many many beautiful things have happened in my life Adam. I don't think it is even possible to mention them all, as there are countless. Allah (SWT) paved my way, I would just meet amazing people all the time and good work would be taken from me, in ways I couldn't have planned for or imagined. I have and AM being used as an instrument of deen.

What can I share with you? Well I have had the good fortune of running a sisters circle in Leeds after attending *Daure Quran* as a student of learning, Allah (swt) enabled that to be a stepping stone, to help me to find a new home in Madni Masjid to be a bridge, which would help to encourage the younger generation to have a stronger relationship with Allah swt house, for them to hold fast onto that rope. I didn't even hunt or look to the Masjid, to find an opportunity, it looked for me and that scared me as well. Who was I to teach or share knowledge to people? What was so special in me that I dared to think I had anything worthy to give to others..?

I just knew that Allah (swt) had made it so easy for me to accept that invitation. I thought I will do one class and we will see and Masha'Allah, Masha'Allah, so many sessions have run in the Masjid, we have had social gatherings, Iftari's, even made some Eid cards for the Palestinian children. Seeing the sisters and the children so happy, it makes all those hours of work and effort worth it.

It would just melt my heart to know that I played a part in welcoming people to enter the House of Allah (swt), what a blessing and a gift to be picked for this role, without hunting or training or aspiring to it. It just came into my life, when Allah (swt) deemed it to be the right time Alhamdulillah.

Other doors have also opened in a similar fashion and I currently find myself as the sole Muslim Chaplain at Leeds University, Masha'Allah. This has been the hardest and most rewarding chapter work wise. I have been pushed on so many levels mentally, morally and spiritually and I seem to be using every tool I have with the university community.

Even you my dear son have been mentioned on a few occasions and thinking back to when I was at your grave on that winters day 5 years ago, for anyone to say to me that in 5 years' time, I would be using those experiences to help heal and soften the pain of others grieving, I just wouldn't be able to believe it. I see tutors, and lecturers, and directors and students of all faith and communities and they seem Masha'Allah so responsive to the help that I am giving.

This chapter is still continuing Adam and I am so grateful to have this opportunity to have this impact at my age. You have inspired me to remember life is short and to take all the chances I have, and not to be scared of trying.

I have tried my hardest to do the work of Allah (SWT) in every-day life, chance meetings, conversations with colleagues, emailing people reflections of what I have learnt every day, to keep you alive in my heart that you are with Allah (SWT) now. That serves as a constant reminder that I don't live in this world, not permanently, and the next life is where I want to be, to live in the palaces of light and jewels and diamonds.

To know that there is a place Allah (SWT) has prepared for us, where there is no pain and suffering anymore, where we can reunite with friends and families of all generations and ultimately to be with our Creator, our Guardian who gives us only what is best for us.

I miss you a lot and the last 5 years feel bearable knowing that one day I will see you again Insha'Allah.

My Adam, your phupie still visits your grave regularly and makes duas for you. Not a single day in 5 years have

I forgotten you and you remain constantly alive in my conversations and actions and reactions to this world. You changed me more than I could say. When you were alive you changed me and now that you have left us, you have changed me.

You make me a better aunt, daughter, sister, human being, that was true when you were amongst us and still remains true now, Allah (SWT) is most Merciful and most Gracious. He knows what's best for me and taking my nephew away from me, to help me to remember my friendship with my Maker, how can that not be a beautiful awakening of the heart and mind.

You are never ever forgotten your name still rings the streets of Bradford and your name is mentioned after so many salahs, still unto this day.

My child let your temporary holding place be filled with Noor (light) and protection and Insha'Allah I will see you soon, I will hug you again one day and I will get a chance to see that amazing smile.

Love you always and forever.

Farhat, (Adam's phuphie)

Assalmu Alaykum,

Life changes you and you can't do anything about it, people come in this world and people go. I always loved you, I know I never said it to you, I don't really say it to anyone that I love them, that's just the way I am, I am doing my best to make our Mum and Dad proud. I just want to be a good Son/Brother and I just want to make everyone happy.

I know I don't talk much, I just want to make a positive effect on this world in some way or form, I know I don't remember you as much as I should it's not that I don't want to, it's just that I am not ready to die yet. I don't think I have done enough in this world to pass THE TEST, I know Allah (SWT) has blessed me very well and I can't complain about life. I just can't thank Him enough and I know I don't say it enough. I know I am not you but I try my best to make everyone happy just like you would, with that little smile on your face you used to have. Over the last few years I have grown up and now have became more mature. I have just finished my last year in University doing a degree just to make our mum happy in memory of you.

Arslan Ayub, (Adams Brother)

Salam,

I feel like it's been a while since I have spoken to you, it's a bit weird that I'm 20 now, getting older and over the last five years so many things have happened. I just want to say that you had a huge impact in my life and I thank Allah for Him putting you in my life as you have taught me so much, Thank you. I know you're in peace and I pray that I will meet you in Jannah Insha'Allah with everyone. So many things are happening, I miss you and love you till the moon and back.

I still remember all the little things you used to do and say. Some things have not changed as you are still the eldest and everyone's favourite. Grandma loves and misses you dearly, every time I go to see her she just speaks about you, the kids still ask me questions about you like *"Did Adam Bhai like this?" "What was Adam Bhai like?"*. You have left a mark in everyone's heart. You are a legend haha, I still wear your jackets, don't get angry, but it looks better on me anyway.

Guess what, you graduated, wohoooo, now Insha'Allah with the will of Allah Arslan will be graduating. It's going to take two years for me but I'm loving university. I'm studying Islam and I'm working at a school, all the little babies running around calling Miss Ambar. I have met some beautiful people recently. Ever since you left I feel like I have grown so much as a person, I know that there is an afterlife and we do need to work for it. As long as I'm going forward to do better things and become a better human being, I'm happy. You have made me realise that nothing lasts forever, which means everything you have you should appreciate it and I expect the unexpected. We passed our driving tests, just thought I would put that in there, since I passed on my first time, not bragging or anything, haha.

Everyone is good Alhamdulillah and we are just taking one step at a time, I don't really think too far ahead of time, I just want to cherish every moment and be constantly busy seeing Allah's world as it just humbles you and you realise that you are a tiny dot and Allah still gives you everything on a plate. It can be hard sometimes because I think what if you was still here and then I realise I shouldn't think like that, the fact that you were in my life for all them years is a blessing itself. Since you have gone I have just opened my eyes so much more as I realised many things internally about myself. Allah has given me three brothers that are all completely different and I love you all.

Insha'Allah see you in heaven,

I love you,

From the most amazing sibling you have, Ambar,

(Adams Sister)

Dear Adam,

I want know how you are. Everyone's grown up. I've grown older. I wanted you to see me grow but I know that cannot happen. I can't wait to see you bro in the Hereafter. Mum said write a letter to you to express my feelings but I feel as though you are never going to read it.

I feel frustrated and wish you were here to guide me in the little things in life as well as the big things. I just want to see you, but Allah has done everything for a reason. I know you're in a better place. The kids thesedays days are idiots, not like you back in the good all days. I loved playing football and fighting (wrestling) with you.

I can never forget you Adam, I love you and I don't want to forget about you. All I think about is the good times we had together and reminisce of the old times, and think of life if you were here but you are gone now. Insha Allah I will see you in the Hereafter. I don't know what to say now, I could write a lot more but I am not good at letters.

Adam you are in my duas.

Love you loads,
Ahmad Ayub, (Adam's youngest brother)

Salaam Adam Bhai,

It has been 5 years since you have passed away. The family miss you so much. It's me Isam who is writing your best younger cousin I miss you too. Two years back Allah (SWT) the Mighty One has blessed us with a beautiful home. When we have katams at your house Phuphie would ask *"who remembers anything about when Adam bhai was here"* we all would say several things and really miss you.

I know now that you are peacefull with Allah (SWT) My mum says we all will be together one day and meet our loved ones. We need to follow the right path and the teachings of Prohet Muhammad (PBUH). We all may do some bad deeds here in this world. We have a strong belief of Islam till we meet again Insha Allah. I always see sadness in Thai Abu's face when you were taken away. My mum says Allah (SWT) needed you more that's why you left us..... May Allah (SWT) bless you with the highest level of Jannat .....Ameen. Gone but never ever ever forgotten.

Khuda Hafiz, Adam Bhai.

(Isam, Adams cousin)

Salaam.

Can't believe it is coming to 6 years since you left us Adam. A lot has happened and changed. My son Muhammad arrived on 31st July 2011 and shortly after my dad returned back to Allah (SWT). Still cannot believe my dad has gone feels so unreal at times. Oh Adam Muhammad is a very funny character not to mention the hyperness he has. Abid your Uncle can't control him he puts him in knots! Zuha lives with the fairies and princesses and Masha'Allah Isam is very towards his Deen.

Isam has started to read Namaz, and also started the Quran Paak too. He makes me so proud that I start crying out of joy. Isam often talks about you and the Hereafter. Honestly after you left us I realised what life is about and how it should be lived. How it could be our last day today. Seeing you leave, had huge effect on lots of people and it's amazing how much change you have brought to people. May Allah (SWT) continue this book and its Sadaqah e Jaria for you...

Love from Aunty Zeenit

Salam my dear brother,
nephew, son and friend Adam.

Its been a while since I have had the opportunity to write to you again. Its been over five years since I have seen you but every day, every second, every minute I never stop thinking about you. Its very hard to forget such an amazing, kind, honest, humble, special human being who bought happiness to so many people even though you were suffering from your illness, you hid your pain, sadness and fear from a lot of people so you could be treated just like any other person.

Allah does everything for a purpose and everybody will one day leave this world and Insha'Allah join him in the world after. Your time was very short but your memories will stay with us until we also make that journey to our creator. I think once you left us, you made a lot of people take account of their own lives and changed their focus, in terms of Deen and also their outlook on life.

We all take things for granted and maybe our Deen takes a backstep in order for us to follow our greed and desire. You showed us that our Deen and Ummah is more important than anything we may need.

Allah can easily take everything away from us as easily as he can give it to us. Doctors told us that you would not survive as long as you did but only Allah can decide that. You touched so many hearts in different ways and your attitudes and courage to life should be an example to us all. I know that you are looking over us and also praying for us all. Insha'Allah I pray we all follow your path and the qualities you had. We need to set examples to our family, friends and Ummah like you did as our time could end at any moment. If that time happens I pray that we are all in position to feel that we can join you in Allah's house and we can only stay strong in our deen and stay focused.

Its time to end this letter but you are constantly in my thoughts and heart. Please keep an eye on all of us and make sure that if we ever stray away from Allah's path you push us back to Allah. My time will come when I will Insh Allah be with you, make sure you have lots of room for all of us.

Khuda hafiz,
Yousaf and family

What have I learnt from my life?

- It is not our eyes but hearts which are blind.

- Everything in this world has a purpose; do not forget yours.
- Offer Salah before people offer Salah for you (the funeral prayer).

- Spread happiness.

- In a real sense, a liberated person is one who is not a slave of his desires.

- Change yourself according to Allah's commands; your fate will change automatically.

- Do not see "who" is saying, but pay attention to "what" is being said.

- If you plan to do a good deed, act before you lose the opportunity to do so.

• There is a big difference between fulfilling your needs and fulfilling your desires.

• The more loaded a tree is with fruit, the more it will bow. In human attitudes this is the fruit of humility.

• If you do not cleanse your heart, it will rust and the heart's rust can only be washed away by remembrance of Allah.

• The state of our hearts has more more effect on us than the outside weather.

• Be true to yourself. Nobody knows you better than Allah. All our excuses are for this world only.

• Judge yourself before you are judged by Allah.

• What preparations have I made for the Hereafter? Are my luggage and handbag full of good deeds and ready?

• Assimilate Qur'an into your being so that your life is successful.

• It only takes a moment to slip. No matter what height man reaches, it doesn't take long for him to fall.

• We must always keep watch over the fortress of our heart; otherwise thieves of jealousy, greed, hurry (Satanic trait), miserliness, fury, religious prejudice and desire for worldly things will enter it and erode this fortress like termites.

• Love is present on the shelves of our heart. The more we love a person, the higher the shelf it will be on. We must tell people how much we love them during their lives.

• Ask Allah for wisdom, for it is a great blessing.

• What, after all, prevents me from getting close to Allah: money, children, desires, this world, this world and again this world?

• Meditate on all of Allah's creations like the sky, birds, fruits, vegetables, trees, oceans, man and animals.

• Continuing to tread the same path will not lead to a different destination. If you aim to reach a different one, then change your path.

• Analyse yourself critically each day because only you know yourself.

• Gratitude eliminates complaints and complaints eliminate gratitude.

• Sacrifice always wins, even if it has to wait for years.

• You cannot teach anything to anyone unless Allah so wills and the man in question want to learn himself.

• Dua is like magic. Try it for yourself.

• Friendship with Allah is priceless. He is that friend of yours who can read what is in your heart without your saying it.

• If a specific Dua of yours does not get fulfilled, rest assured it is better for you.

• If something happens in life which you never expected, understand that Allah will make it easy for you even if you never had wished for it.

• When things go against your wishes, take it that they have happened on Allah's command and you have to be patient.

•   If you get a chance to help someone, be aware that Allah has made you a means to do so in answer to that person's Dua, Praise be to Allah.

•   Every step that I take towards goodness will make me distant from evil. So before taking any step, consider carefully whether it will take you towards good or bad. Because if your distance decreases from one side, then it is bound to increase from the other.

•   Our children are Allah's best gift. We must give them a superb upbringing and transfer our knowledge of religion to the next generation, because religion is something which we have also inherited and must pass on.

•   Any respect or service you give to someone will never go waste, even if you do not see its result immediately.

•   This world is an examination centre where there is no time to relax and rest. Remember, no test is without a result.

•   Imaan makes man more sensitive towards his own self and towards the world as well.

•   Momin fears Allah, not the law, whereas an ordinary person is scared of worldly law but not Allah.

•   Make your children fear Allah (Taqwa) and not you.

•   Help others only for Allah's sake, not for your own benefit.

•   Abstain from your sins in such a way that you begin to detest evil as though you never liked it.

•   Hold on to patience during sorrow and joy, because patience guarantees success in life.

• Taqwa (fear of Allah) and patience go hand in hand.

• Do not go even close to the boundaries set by Allah. Make your Imaan so strong that even if you find yourself near these boundaries, you are able to save yourself from erring.

• Allah's blessings cannot be seen, but only felt.

• We must keep cleansing our hearts just like we clean our faces.

• Our standard is the Qur'an, not people.

• Good deeds demand sacrifice.

• He who is not grateful to people is not grateful to Allah.

• When we collect good deeds it is as though we are collecting riches for Aakhirah (Hereafter).

• A Momin is like a wall (support) for another Momin.

• Qur'an dispels all the darkness of heart and enlightens it.

• Care about people. Allah will take care of you.

• Rearing children is like gardening. You will reap what you sow.

• During trying times, the biggest test is that of our faith. So take special care of it in difficult times.

• Children can be Sadaqa e Jariya or a trial for you.

• Heaven is surrounded by difficulties and sacrifices whereas Hell is surrounded by desires.

• Actions require knowledge.

• If you are desirous of Allah's forgiveness, then learn to forgive people

• Qiyamah (Day of Judgement) will be a day of wishing and yearning when man will wish that he had built a better house for himself in the hereafter.

• Learn to trust in Allah because He never shuts His doors.

• Keep checking the frequency of your good deeds and sins.

• Keep connecting people with Allah.

• Husband and wife are each other's clothing. So safeguard and value your clothes.

• There are signs in the sky and earth for those who think.

• Momin are apprehensive even after doing a good deed whether it will be accepted or not by Allah.

• Keep lighting candles so that when your candle blows out someone else may light a candle of knowledge and good deeds.

• Be patient about all that you do not get in this world. You will get it in the hereafter In Sha Allah.

• Muslims are examples of those trees which bear fruit in every season and benefit others.

• Satan is our open enemy who is not incarcerated.

- If Allah forbids us from doing something, do we obey Him?

- There is no compromise in religion.

- We ask for Allah's blessings and bounties, but we do not do anything to deserve them.

- Remembrance of Allah is a full time job, not a part time one.

- Learn to value time and do not waste it, for we cannot bring back even a moment of the past.

- Pray for this world and for the hereafter too.

- Satan disobeyed Allah by refusing to prostrate once; how many times in a day do we disobey Allah and refrain from prostrating?

- Do not make insignificant things important; otherwise important things will become insignificant.

- Give importance to your preferences.

- A Momin speaks more with heart than tongue.

- Life, like a slab of ice, is melting quickly.

- The person who does not help others is like a flower with no fragrance.

- Our today must be better than our yesterday.

- Allah's blessings are uncountable, then why do we count money when spending in His name?

- To pardon someone is the best example of patience.

- Hate the sin not the sinner.

- The pride of knowledge is the biggest pride of all.

- Understanding of Qur'an changes one's thinking and thinking changes his actions.

- When you see anything evil, it is much easier to chop it off and throw it away, but a lot more difficult to remain connected to it and try to put it right. The latter is a cause for big reward from Allah.

- Practising patience when you are first hit is most rewarding. Time itself is a healer and brings patience with it anyway.

- Imaan gives insight to man.

- To admit one's mistake is a sign of Imaan.

- A single word uttered by the tongue can take a person to the highest level of Heaven or the deepest pit of Hell.

- People do not see what Allah sees, that is, our good deeds. And Allah does not see what selfish people see, that is, our external beauty and riches, etc.

- The greatness of elders depends on being open-minded and big-hearted.

- Truth leads to virtuous deeds.

- This world is a path leading towards the Hereafter, not a destination.

- Keeping order in one's life is very important.

- Allah grants man according to man's expectation of Allah. So always have high hopes and expectations from your Creator.

- Qur'an is a treasure whereas Imaan is our possessions.

- Refrain from idle talk.

- Reflect daily on what you did today.

- Associate with people in such a way that they pray for you on their own without you having to request it.

- A drop of practice is better than a sea of knowledge.

- Daily, I forget Allah's favours and He forgets my mistakes.

- Words like "if" and "if only" open doors to Satan.

- It does not suit a Muslim to be on the righteous path himself and not invite others towards this path.

- Gratitude and being satisfied with what you've got are two of Allah's great bounties.

- There is a difference between arrogance and self-confidence. It is very important to know this difference.

- We safeguard our money in the world, whereas Qur'an protects us in this world as well as in the Hereafter.

- A son is Allah's blessing and a daughter is Allah's mercy.

- Supplication (Dua) is a prayer.

- Each breath is more precious than the most precious diamond.

- Life is meant for great actions and deeds, not small and insignificant actions.

- Value time and make the best use of it.

- Noble deeds are our capital for the Hereafter. Collect as many of them as you can.

- Religion should be like our own business and we should be as concerned about it as we are with our worldly businesses.

- Help others and be extravagant in your prayers.

- Time is like a diamond. Do not exchange a diamond for a stone; make good use of your time.

- A Momin does not require praise or any repayment from people. He performs good and noble deeds only for the sake of Allah.

- Knowledge which gets stolen is not true knowledge. Real knowledge is that which assimilates in you and is reflected in your actions.

- We will not be able to do anything for our religion nor find peace of mind until we forgive others.

- All our battles are for our own selves. We do not fight any battle for our religion anymore.

- Refrain from undue questions.

- People want to change the world, but are not ready to change themselves.

- We cannot hope to be entirely free of Shirk until we break the idols of egotism and desires.

- Gratitude makes you realise all that Allah has given you whereas thanklessness makes you think about what you lack.

- Life is not only joviality and laughter.

- Remembrance of Allah is a Momin's shield.

- Do not be so dependent on people anymore and they will begin to love you.

- Man is such a pathetic planner that he never includes his death in any of his plans.

- The month of Ramadhan is actually the "month of sale for good deeds", because Satan is confined during this time and you can increase your good deeds manifold - fifty times, seventy times, one hundred times or seven hundred times.

- If you meditate on the universe you will understand the Oneness of Allah.

- Everything which is a burden on our ego is Jihad.

- A Momin always learns from his and others' mistakes.

- It is necessary to listen carefully before you learn anything.

- Religion and the world are not two separate things. Religion is everything and we have to attain the world through it.

- Keep a strict check on your intentions all the time.

- One must be worried about one's house in the Hereafter

and its decoration.

• The Sunnah of Prophet Muhammad (PBUH) is like Noah's Ark. All those who get into it will be saved and those left behind will be ruined.

• Allah will not accept the Dua of those who thrive on prohibited (Haraam) money.

• The worst deity is man's ego.

• Religious people are large hearted and they forgive others.

• Allah is the best painter and the whole universe is Allah's canvas.

• Jealousy burns and kills its owner before his natural death.

• Do not make the world your concern. Your concern should be the Hereafter.

• Wake up from the slumber of ignorance.

• We are the inheritors of Qur'an. Are we fulfilling our duty towards it?

• One thinks of bad deeds again and again, but not about good ones. So whenever you think of or plan to do good, act on it immediately.

• The war within oneself is tougher than the one outside.

• Give value and respect to everyone in life, because a good person will make you happy and a bad person will teach you a lesson.

- If knowledge is not supported by action, it will be taken away.

- It is easy to wander on paths of sin.

- When we offer Salah we talk to Allah, and when we recite Qur'an, Allah talks to us.

- *"I like the person amongst you who has good behaviour."* (Hadeeth e Nabvi).

- The knowledge of Islam is like rain. If we do not absorb the rain, this knowledge will not benefit us.
- Imaan strengthens you from within, not outside.

- Marriage is our Prophet's way; it is a contract and is equal to half of our Imaan.

- Music can never be the food for our souls, but Allah's remembrance is the food for our souls.

- Intention converts a habit into a prayer.

- You can never please people by displeasing Allah.

- Taqwah teaches you to fear Allah not people.

- Be concerned for yourselves and change your actions accordingly. We cannot change others. Only Allah can modify people's hearts.

- Anything coming from the heart is bound to reach others' hearts and affect them, whereas hollow words of the tongue will only reach the ears and have no effect.

- Modesty and Imaan are friends. If one goes the other

leaves too.

• Imaan is the belief of heart, expression of tongue and testimony by actions.

• Allah does not like quarrelsome and argumentative people.

• The world is colourful for people without Imaan (Kaafir).

• Loss of respect and esteem in a man is like the breaking of the beads of a Tasbeeh (rosary).

• Adopt such behaviour with people that whoever meets you once would like to meet you again.

• Only a Allah-fearing person can practise patience.

• Take decisions based on Allah's commands, not on emotions.

• There is no mischief greater than a woman. On the other hand, a man's best possession is a virtuous wife.

• We make a lot of preparations for a baby's entry into the world, but forget to make preparations for his departure.

• A Momin finds opportunities to do good deeds and keeps an eye on his time.

• Make your near and dear ones feel your presence or else time will teach them to live without you.

• Trust that person who understands these three traits of you: sorrow behind your smile, love behind your anger, the reason behind your silence.

• A Momin lives his life between the feelings of fear and

hope.

•   Include those "friends" in your life who remain by your side in the form of a mirror or a shadow, because a mirror never lies and a shadow does not leave you ever.

•   The colour of our blood is the same whether we are Hindus, Christians, Sikhs or Muslims.

•   Learn to endure, keep your tongue under control and persevere.

•   A good deed is one which gives pleasure and peace to man and sin is that which makes man restless.

•   Pardon is a good revenge, whereas silence is the best punishment.

•   Good deeds give longevity to life and radiance to the face.

•   Trial by one's conscience is the toughest trial on earth.

•   Difficult times test one's conscience.

•   Every person who shakes your hand is not your friend.

•   Those who forget their dear ones will not remember outsiders for long either.

•   Silence enhances a man's dignity.

•   Be moderate in your love and hatred so that you do not have to face embarrassment.

•   Our tongue gives us respect and is also a cause of defamation.

- Feelings and emotions never age.

- Do not hasten to take revenge and do not delay good gestures.

- Do not spend your life in search of a good person; instead, become a good person yourself so that other peoples' search comes to an end.

- The faces of truthful people do not lie.

- Do not leave any relationship incomplete in life because incomplete relations scratch and injure your soul like pieces of broken glass.

- Half-truths are more dangerous than full lies.

- The servants of Rahman walk the earth with humility.

- Allah (SWT) does not like hardness of tongue. That is why there is no bone in the tongue.

- Truth which is spoken spontaneously is better than a planned lie.

- Good behaviour is a shop and the tongue is its lock. Only when you open the lock will you know whether the shop is of gold or coal.

- Be soft in your conversation because your manner of speech has more impact than your words.

- We are nothing without Allah's help, and with his help we can do anything and everything.

- Think positively and speak well, because suspicion and rough language are errors which destroy all the talents of man.

- When life shuts its doors, man begins to realise his mistakes, but the time to correct oneself or do good deeds is gone.

- If your relationships are sincere, you will not have to toil to maintain them. While those that require a lot of effort to keep going are not sincere.

- Do not delay asking for forgiveness from Allah because death comes without warning.

- Safeguarding your tongue is more difficult than safeguarding your money.

- Imaan is a seed and Momin is a tree.

- When a person enters the circle of Islam, Allah tests him.

- The most useful act which benefits a man is his/her own good deeds.

- There is much difference between a man of knowledge and a man of action.

- If you plan to sin, do it somewhere outside Allah's kingdom.

- Momin is a fine tree who benefits other people as well.

- To forgive someone is the best revenge.

- A woman's silence is her language.

- Stubbornness destroys everything. Whatever is left behind does not provide peace either.

- Without Imaan, children and money will be of no benefit either in world or in the hereafter.

- To have trust in Allah is a greatest blessing.

- To pardon someone is also a Sadaqah.

- A man's speech reveals him from inside and outside.

- A Momin never despairs because hopelessness is Kufar.

- Man's biggest enemy is his ego.

- A mother is a fragrance which fills the whole world with her beautiful scent.

- One has to pass the test of love so that love is proven. This applies to love for Allah as well as for people.

- Imaan and Kufr cannot co-exist.

- Leaving the house to do something noble is Hijrah (migration).

- A Muslim is one who believes in Allah, a Momin is one who obeys Allah.

- Man is afraid of death but cannot evade it and he is not scared of Hell, though he can avoid it.

- When we do not obey Allah, then our children do not obey us either.

- It is difficult to climb up the stairs and easy to climb down. Similarly, it is difficult to go towards good deeds and easy to go towards sin.

- Lifeless things have a long life but man's life is limited.

- People lie so easily and fluently that they do not even

realise it.

• Love is a sentiment of the heart. What you get by force is not love, but compromise.

• When a person acquires experience in this world, he has to retire. When he understands life, then it is time for him to depart.

• Knowledge and success are only paths, not destinations.

• Keep collecting pearls of sincerity and faith and you will stay clear of the thorns of hatred.

Final Words

Oh my Rabb, "Rahman and Raheem" (the most Merciful and the most Benevolent), an insignificant person like me has written this book to gain your favours. Oh my Creator, I bow before You in gratitude that you enabled me to write something. Oh Allah (SWT), if due to my meagre knowledge or unintentionally, I have written something which clashes with Your commands or is against the teachings of our beloved Prophet (PBUH), I seek Your forgiveness from the core of my heart and ask for Your special blessings.

Oh *Wahhab* (one who grants to all)! Please pardon my unimportant being, my husband, my children, my in-laws, parents, brothers, sisters, my associates and all the Muslims. Please make this book *Sadaqa e Jariya* for me, my family, its readers and my beloved deceased son Muhammad Adam Ayub, Ameen. Oh Lord, please give the best reward to all the people for their efforts who helped me to make this project possible, Ameen.

In the end I thank my Allah (SWT) who chose me for this work with my entire being. I am thankful to my husband, without whose love and encouragement, I would not have been able to complete this project. Praise be to Allah , my parents' prayers were with me at every step, and my children made me proud throughout the entire task. It is my humble request to all the readers that, as a poet said:

337

Oh, friend erase all your complaints before sleeping
Death does not have to make an appointment to meet you

And finally:

When will my life come to an end I don't know
Pardon me for any hurt that I might have caused

(Urfana Ayub)

I am free

Don't grieve for me, for now I'm free,
I'm following paths Allah made for me
I took his hand I heard him call
Then turned, and bid farewell to all

I could not stay another day
To laugh, to love, to sing, to play
Tasks left undone must stay that way

I found my peace... at close of play

And if my parting left a void
Then fill it with remembered joy
A friendship shared, a laugh, a kiss
Ah yes, these things I too will miss.

Be not burdened... deep with sorrow
I wish you sunshine of tomorrow
My life's been full I've savoured much
Good friends, good times
A loved one's touch

Perhaps my time seemed all too brief
Don't lengthen it now with grief
Lift up your hearts and share with me,
Allah wants me now... He set me free.

Anonymous

Editor's Note

Five years after the death of her beloved son Adam, Urfana shares the wisdom and faith she has gained since his passing to bring solace to readers on the same journey.

Her life experience combines with her work as a counsellor to produce a book that is spiritual, lyrical and full of common sense advice on nurturing human relationships and living a meaningful life.

Siobhan Dignan

Acknowledgements

A tremendous thank you to my family near and far, who remain my strength and without whom neither I nor any of my writing would have been possible.

Thank you Ayub, my husband and my dear friend, who held my hand through every moment of writing this and after. Without his support and encouragement I could not have completed this book. Thank you Ayub, whose optimism and spirit kept me going and who had faith in me as I began this journey.

Thank you to someone very special who wants to remain anonymous, but who is dear to me, and whose support and trust in me was invaluable at every step in making this book a reality. After Allah (SWT), she was my greatest strength and assistance to fulfil my dream.

Thank you all my Urdu readers for your encouragement and feedback and for giving me the confidence and motivation to take this step.

Thank you Dr Samira, Dr Zahid, Siobhan, Arslan, Ahmad, Ambar, Maria, Usman and my parents whose contribution, support and duas have nurtured this book.

Above all, Allah (SWT) has given me this opportunity, and I can never repay my son Mohammad Adam Ayub who is the reason behind these books. May Allah (SWT) grant him Jannat ul Firdous Ameen.

Urfana Ayub

About the Author

Mrs. Urfana Ayub was born in Karachi (Pakistan), now settled in Bradford, UK since 1990. As a qualified Social Worker, Interpreter, Translator and Counsellor, she is actively engaged with people, their problems and emotions. This work has enabled her to see life very closely and given her a wider experience of the problems faced by families and their reactions. At the same time her profession has also given her the insight to see beyond the *"outer face"*, into the souls of others. All these experiences have added depth to Urfana's writing. Her command of language and expression are proof of the effects of her profession, as she has never written before in her life.

Urfana Ayub possesses a very positive personality and has the rare talent of seeing good in every person and situation. This quality has helped her immensely to bear the tragedy of losing her son and redirect her life on a new path.

Glossary

10th of Muharram - A day of great significance in Islam, including being the day of martyrdom of Hussain (RA), the grandson of Prophet Muhammad (PBUH), along with his family and clan.

Aab e Zam Zam - The holy water obtained from the holy well of Zam Zam in Makkah.

Aalim - Literally means anyone who has knowledge, used specifically for people who have had religious education.

Aalima - Feminine of Aalim

Aamil - Literally means "doer" or "factor". The term used for someone who performs (or claims he does so) certain rituals or recitations to make things happen.

Abba - A title used for father but can also be put after the title for another male relation one or two generations older like Nana or Dada etc.

Abbu - A title used for one's father, but in this book also used for my father-in-law. Also see Abba

Abu Bakr - A Sahabi (companion) of Holy Prophet (PBUH) who was the first among men to become a Muslim and was the first Khalifah (Caliph) after the Holy Prophet (PBUH).

Abu Huraira -A Sahabi of Prophet Muhammad (PBUH) who

343

is quoted as source of many of the Ahadeeth.

Ahadeeth - Plural of Hadith.

Ahle Kitab - Literally meaning people having the book of scriptures, mostly referring to Jews and Christians.

Ahram - The un-sewn sheets men wrap to perform Hajj or Umrah.

Allahamdulilah - Literally meaning "All praise be to Allah (SWT)", but often used to express thanks to Allah (SWT).

Ali (Hazrat) - First cousin and son-in-law of Prophet Muhammad (PBUH) who was the fourth Khalifah of the Muslims.

Allah'Hafiz - The words used in farewell, meaning "May Allah be your protector".

Allahu Akbar - Translation: "Allah (SWT) is the greatest".

Ameen - The Arabic pronunciation of Amen

Ammi - 1. Alone this title is used for one's mother, but in this book it also refers in most places to my mother-in-law, who is like a mother to me. 2. It can also be used as a suffix with a title for a female relative one or two generations older like Dadi, Nani etc.

Ashraf-ul-Makhlooqat - The most superior creation (of Allah (SWT), meaning the human race.

Asr - The obligatory prayer offered between mid afternoon and sunset (3rd Prayer).

Peace be upon you - Muslim greeting meaning "May peace be upon you".

Astaghfirullah - "I ask for the forgiveness of Allah."

Baba - Literally meaning old man, but affectionate title used sometimes for father and sometimes for grandfather; in this book used mostly for my father-in-law and Adam's grandfather.

Baraat - Marriage procession consisting of groom's near and dear ones who accompany the groom to the bride's home where they are entertained by her family.

Bhabhi - Brother's wife

Bhai - Brother

Bukhari - One of the books making up the collection of Ahadeeth.

Bullhey Shah - A famous mystic poet born in Uch (Pakistan) and buried in Kasur (Pakistan).

Chachcha - Father's younger brother

Chachchi - Chachcha's wife

Dada - Paternal grandfather

Dadi - Paternal grandmother

Dawood (prophet) - Prophet David

Deen - Religion

Dua - Supplication

Eid - One of the two occasions in Islamic calendar to celebrate.

Eid ul Ad'ha - Religious festival of the Muslims, celebrated on 10th of Zilhaj -the last month of Islamic calendar.

Eid ul Fitr - Religious festival observed by Muslims, celebrated at the end of the Holy Month of Ramadhan.

Ghazali - 11th century Muslim theologian and philosopher born in Iran.

Hadith - Literally means "anything which has been said", but is the Islamic term for the sayings of Holy Prophet (PBUH).

Hadith e Qudsi - A Hadith of Prophet Muhammad (PBUH) which is a direct quote of Allah's (SWT) words.

Hadhrat - A title of respect put before the names of Prophets, companions of the Prophet Muhammad (PBUH), or any holy person.

Hajj - One of the five pillars of Islam, referring to the sacred rituals performed in and around Makkah once a year. Performing Hajj is mandatory at least once in a lifetime for every Muslim who has means to do so.

Hamd - Literally means praise, but the term is denoted specifically for the poetry praising Allah (SWT).

Imaan - Belief, faith

Imran - Believed to be the name of Mary's father.

Insha'Allah - Literally meaning "if Allah (SWT) wills", used when one is hoping and praying from Allah (SWT).

Isha - The prayer offered about one and a half hours after sunset when the darkness has set in (5th/Final Prayer of the day).

Heaven - Paradise

Jannat ul Firdaus - One of the highest places in paradise

Jazak'Allah - May Allah (SWT) reward you

Jihad - Literally means "effort", but in Islam means making the effort in the path of Allah (SWT). This includes but is not limited to fighting with the non-Muslim for the sake of Allah (SWT).

Kaa'ba - The holy pilgrimage place in Makkah where Muslims go to perform Hajj or Umrah.

Kafan - Shroud

Kafir - Non-believer

Kalimah (Shahadah) - One of the five pillars of Islam meaning "There is no Allah but Allah, Muhammad (Peace be Upon Him) is his messenger".

Khala - Mother's sister

Khalifah - Caliph

La Illaha IllAllah - "There is no Allah but Allah (SWT)." (see Kalimah)

Luqman Hakeem - Believed to be Aesop

Masha'Allah - Literally meaning "As Allah wills". Used to praise something and pray for Allah's protection for it at the same time.

Madinah - Literally meaning city, but now the name of the city where Prophet Muhammad (PBUH) spent the last decade of his life and is buried therein.

Madrassah - Literally meaning school, but specifically refers to school for religious education.

Maghrib - The prayer offered just after sunset (4th Salah).

Makkah - The birthplace of Prophet Muhammad (PBUH), the city where the Kaaba is where the Muslim go for Hajj.

Mamoon & Mumani - Mother's brother & his wife

Masjid - Mosque

Masjid e Nabvi - The Holy Mosque, initially built by Prophet Muhammad (PBUH) in Madina.

Momin - Believer

Muharram - The first month of the Islamic calendar

Muslim (book) - One of the books containing a collection of Ahadeeth compiled by Muslim Ibn al Hajjaj.

Musnad Ahmad - One of the books containing a collection of Ahadeeth

Namaz - Salah or prayer.

Nana - Maternal grandfather

Nand - Husband's sister

Nani - Maternal grandmother

Nauzobillah - Literally meaning "we ask for the protection of Allah (SWT)". Roughly equates to "Allah forbid".

Nasai - One of the books containing a collection of Ahadeeth

Peer - Persian word for old person, but can also be a term used for saints.

Phuphie - Father's sister

Qabar -Grave

Qur'an - The holy book of Allah (SWT) revealed to Muhammad (PBUH).

RA - Short for *Razi Allah o Taala Unhu*, meaning: "May Allah (SWT) be pleased with him", a title used for the companions of Prophet Muhammad (PBUH).

Ramadhan - The ninth month of the Islamic calendar during which the Muslim observe fasting.

Rauza - Mausoleum

Sadaqa e Jariya - A good deed performed by someone which keeps on benefiting an individual or the wider community on a permanent basis and becomes a source of eternal reward from Allah (SWT).

Sahaba - Plural of Sahabi

Sahabi - A companion of Prophet Muhammad (PBUH); plural is Sahaba.

Salah - Prayer. Often referred to in Urdu as Namaz.

Shahadah - Meaning both "evidence" and "martyrdom".

Shaheed - Martyr

Shaitan - Satan

Shirk - Literally means sharing. In Islam it means ascribing partners to Allah (SWT) either in person or in His qualities, worship of anyone or anything other than Allah (SWT).

Shuhada - Plural of Shaheed

Subhan'Allah - Glory be to Allah (SWT)

Sunnah - Literally means routine/habit/tradition/rule, but in Islam it refers to Sunnah (way of life) of the Prophet Muhammad (PBUH).

Sunnan Abi Majah - One of the books containing a collection of Ahadeeth.

Surah - A chapter of Qur'an.

SWT - Subhana wa Ta'alla meaning "the Glorified and Almighty".

Takbeer - Means "magnifying", but used for any words uttered to express the greatness of Allah (SWT).

Takbeer-e-Tehreema - Translation: "the Takbeer which prohibits". Refers to saying "Allahu Akbar" at the beginning of Salah, after which certain things like talking etc. become prohibited and remain so until one finishes the Salah.

Tasbeeh -Rosary beads/Prayer beeds.

Tawaf - Circling around

Tirmidhzi - One of the books containing a collection of Ahadeeth

Umar - Sahabi of Prophet Muhammad (PBUH) and second Khalifah of the Muslim

Ummah - Followers/community

Umrah - Sacred rituals, which are offered in and around Makkah and can be offered any time around the year.

Zakat - One of the five pillars of Islam. The faithful donate to charity 2.5% of their possessions/material assets once a year.

Zikr - Remembrance of Allah (SWT)

Adams Photos

1996, Adam (Age 5)
With younger brother Arslan (Age 2)

Adam with younger brother Arslan

Adam with younger brother Arslan

2007, Adam (Age 16)

Adam (Age 17)

Adam (Age 17)

Adam (Age 18)

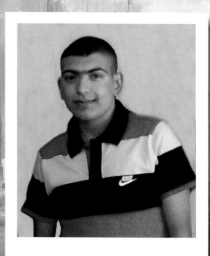

Adam (Age 18)

2009 Adam (Age 18)

"Stars can't shine without darkness"

Adam Ayub Publications

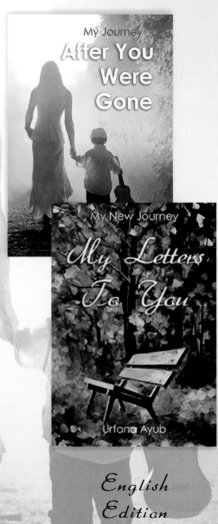

Urdu
Edition

English
Edition